THE DAVID HUME INSTITUTE

Hume Papers on Public Policy
Volume 4 No 2 Spring 1996

FINANCING DEVOLUTION

David Bell, Sheila Dow, David King and Neil Massie

VIVENDO·DISCIMUS

EDINBURGH UNIVERSITY PRESS

Contributors

David Bell is a Professor of Economics at the University of Stirling

Sheila Dow is a Professor of Economics at the University of Stirling

David King is a Senior Lecturer in Economics at the University of Stirling

Neil Massie is a Research Assistant in Economics at the University of Stirling

© David Hume Institute 1996

Edinburgh University Press
22 George Square, Edinburgh

Typeset in Times New Roman by WestKey Limited,
Falmouth, Cornwall
Printed and bound in Great Britain by Page Bros. Limited, Norwich

A CIP record for this book is available from the British Library

ISBN 0 7486 0882 6

Contents

Foreword

The political debate as to the merits and possible shape of devolved government in Scotland has been going on for some time. Following the Kilbrandon
Report (1973), firm proposals emerged in the Scotland Act 1978 but these
failed to command sufficient support in the Referendum of 1979. After a period
of quiet the issue again returned to public prominence under the auspices of
the Scottish Constitutional Convention. If successful at the next election, the
Labour Party is committed to taking a proposal to the Scottish people for a
devolved Scottish Assembly along the lines proposed in the Constitutional
Convention. This proposal will be the subject of a referendum in Scotland.

Although much energy has gone into the detailed discussions regarding these
latest proposals for devolved government in Scotland, relatively little time has
been spent on the nitty gritty detail of how such a layer of government is to
finance the operation of its devolved responsibilities. In this issue of **Hume
Papers on Public Policy** David Bell, Sheila Dow, David King and Neil Massie
pool their expertise to provide a wide ranging and integrated account of the
complexities involved in financing devolution. This work first took shape as a
report to the Constitution Unit earlier this year and provided some of the
background to the Unit's report on the mechanics of establishing a Scottish
Assembly (June 1996). The Constitution Unit's Draft Report was the subject
of a seminar held under the auspices of this Institute on 28 May 1996, the
proceedings of which have been published as **Hume Occasional Paper** No 49.
The Institute is pleased to acknowledge financial support from the Esmée
Fairbairn Charitable Trust for these and other planned publications on the
subject of devolution.

In this extended and developed version of their work, the authors provide a
summary of previous attempts at devolved government in the UK, with
particular attention being paid to the case of Northern Ireland. The all-
important Barnett Formula that plays such a crucial part in determining the
current Block Grant that flows to Scotland is examined in some detail and
scepticism expressed with regard to its ability to survive devolution. The
possible mechanisms by which a Scottish Assembly might raise funds through
tax finance are discussed. Tax assignment has enjoyed some success in Germany and this possibility is reviewed. Whatever its attractions, allowing tax
assignment to a Scottish Assembly presents central government with a possible
loss of fiscal control, although simulation results discussed by the authors

make it clear that the currently proposed range of up to three pence in the pound variation in the standard rate of income tax is unlikely to have any immediate cataclysmic effect on the Scottish economy. Nevertheless, the authors are keen that the advantages to Scotland of the alternative mechanism of tax finance, namely revenue sharing, not be overlooked.

In confronting the likely arrangement for grant finance, which will probably remain the most important source of funding to any Scottish Assembly, the authors provide a detailed account of the current arrangements in terms of grant support to local authorities. Both the timing and the basis of any needs assessment involved will be of crucial importance in the event of devolution. Even if it is accepted that needs rather than crude population numbers should remain the basis for such calculations, there remain vital questions as to exactly how needs are to be set or gauged. An argument is put forward for entrusting such computations to an independent body as happens in Australia. But here, as in the subsequent discussion of the possibility of debt financing, there emerges a considerable potential problem of interaction between an Assembly and the Scottish local authorities. Conflict is likely to arise over subsidiarity, and there is certainly scope for an Assembly to force spending and taxing issues onto local authorities as a consequence of the Assembly's own priorities and actions.

The various chapters in this issue of **Hume Papers on Public Policy** serve as a caution to those who can see no further than the next general election or, if it occurs, any subsequent referendum. There is a considerable amount of detail that remains to be determined with regard to exactly how a devolved Scotland is to be financed and as to what transition arrangements must be set in place to get us from where we are to that new state – should such a change come to be implemented. The authors provide an immensely useful survey of the issues involved and not a few useful pointers as to how they might be resolved.

The David Hume Institute is always pleased to publish work which contributes to public policy issues in such a timely way and which extends the debate already visited in a previous Hume Paper, *Scotland and the Union* 1994 Vol 2 No 2 . That said, the views expressed herein are those of the authors alone, and not of the Institute which as a charity has no collective view or policy line on such questions. But we have no hesitation in commending the work of these authors to the scrutiny of our readership in the safe knowledge that it will add usefully to the debate on this important issue of financing devolution.

Hector L MacQueen and
Brian G M Main
Directors
The David Hume Institute

1 Introduction

Some form of devolved government is likely to be established in the UK if there is a change of government at the next General Election. The Labour Party has committed itself to a devolved Assembly in Scotland within its first year of office. Specific proposals for Scotland have been developed by the Scottish Constitutional Convention, which represents a number of bodies including both the Labour Party and the Liberal Democrats. Both of these parties are considering the extension of devolution to Wales and possibly to the regions of England.

The success and stability of devolved government will depend on the creation of a resourcing mechanism which is acceptable to both national and devolved governments. The Constitutional Convention's proposals for financing devolution are for a combination of block grant and power to vary the standard rate of income tax by up to 3p in the pound. But these proposals have been couched in broad terms, particularly with respect to the block grant. They do not provide an adequate foundation for legislation. They only offer a start to the process of designing suitable financing arrangements, rather than a definitive conclusion.

It is the purpose of this report to take the discussion of financing arrangements several stages further, pointing out the implications of proposals already made and spelling out areas where additional decisions will be required. The main focus is on Scotland where the first devolved Assembly is likely to be established, and where discussions on its implementation are most advanced. However, the Scottish model will inevitably affect any subsequent plans for England and Wales.

An additional complicating factor is that delay or cancellation of the implementation of devolution in England and Wales will result in a possibly indefinite period of asymmetry in the system of government across different parts of the UK, with England and Wales having two layers of government – central and local, while Scotland will have a third layer in the form of an Assembly. Such asymmetry will itself cause problems and, where possible, the report comments on these.

The likelihood that additional Assemblies will quickly follow the Scottish prototype will influence the legislation establishing the Scottish Assembly. If it is to be the first of many, then the structures put in place for the Scottish Assembly must be capable of being generalised elsewhere in the UK. This is particularly true of the financing arrangements. Excessive generosity to

Scotland may limit resources to English or Welsh Assemblies in a way which is generally perceived as unfair. If the Scottish model will not or can not be replicated elsewhere, then the need to provide a general financing mechanism is less pressing.

Thus, though the Constitutional Convention's proposals are likely to provide a starting point for the design of the devolution legislation, other possibilities will also be considered here. A more wide-ranging discussion of financing arrangements will throw new light on the Convention's proposals and encourage a more detailed review. This report is offered as a contribution to this process.

An appropriate starting point for this broader perspective is to consider the main issues raised in previous debates on devolution in the UK. These are considered in Chapter 2, while Chapter 3 addresses issues of the powers to be exercised by devolved Assemblies. Any discussion of financing arrangements can not be divorced from more general discussion of the purpose of devolution. To be effective, funding arrangements will have to be tailored to the functions which they will support. How they reflect the balance of power between levels of government with respect to taxation and spending will also influence their success. Decisions on taxation and spending at one level of government will have both economic and political repercussions on other levels.

The Convention suggests that the Scottish Assembly should be funded primarily by a block grant. Its size will determine spending in key areas of public policy such as health, education, transport and housing. The current 'block' – the funds allocated to the Scottish Office – is determined principally by variants of the so-called Barnett formula. However, in practice, some of the territorial allocation is determined by arrangements which allow spending to bypass the formula. The current funding system is thus not entirely transparent. This permits flexibility in dealing with situations where strict adherence to the Barnett formula would create anomalies with embarrassing political consequences. As a means of resourcing an Assembly, a block grant would have to be transparent since it would effectively be a formal arrangement between two governments. Thus, formula bypass would no longer be an option. This and other issues related to the Barnett formula are explored in Chapter 4.

The Convention proposes to supplement the block grant with revenues from an additional 3 pence in the pound on the standard rate of income tax levied in Scotland only. The reasoning behind this proposal is considered in Chapter 5 in the light of a more wide-ranging discussion of tax powers for devolved government. In particular, the possibility of tax assignment is considered. There are logistical issues associated both with variation in UK tax rates and with assignment of particular taxes, not least the capacity to identify tax revenue by region. There are also issues of principle arising from the division of power between Westminster and regional Assemblies with respect to changing the tax structure. If Westminster were to retain this power (other than some agreed upon variation, such as the three points of income tax) then any change in tax structure agreed in Westminster could have repercussions for the Assemblies' tax revenues. Consideration would therefore have to be given, in designing the financial arrangements for devolution, to whether and how compensation should be given to regional Assemblies for changes in revenues arising from changes in tax policy.

Grant finance is considered in Chapter 6. Consistent application of the Barnett formula will eventually lead to convergence in per capita spending on public services in all the territories. A more generally accepted principle of fairness is funding according to 'need'; the presumption being that per capita needs differ between regions.

In a needs-based approach, the block grant is determined by a comprehensive assessment of both the need for services such as health, education etc. and the cost of their provision. An elaborate needs assessment system is used to determine local authority financing in England and Wales. It would seem strange to continue with such an approach at local authority level but to ignore it for the newly created Assemblies. If such a system is implemented, recent experience with local authorities and the 1979 Treasury needs assessment exercise provides some experience on which to build.

Existing needs assessments have a well-defined scope in terms of the areas where public sector provision is politically acceptable. The legislative powers of a devolved Assembly raise the possibility of differences between Central Government and Assemblies on the range of public sector provision. This implies no agreement between Central Government and the Assembly as to what needs to assess. To avoid this, some method for dealing with changes in the scope of public sector provision covered by the block grant, whether instigated by the Assembly or by Central Government, must be included in the legislation.

A third possible source of funding along with the block grant and tax revenues is borrowing by the regional Assemblies. Even if the aim was to balance the regional budget, interim borrowing power will almost certainly be required to cover any mismatch between revenue and expenditure. But, more significantly, it may prove impossible to design financial arrangements which ensure that spending does not exceed revenue over the entire financial year. The danger of such an outcome is increased, the greater the tendency to opt for a simple block grant which makes no allowance for unforeseen contingencies. In addition, the Assembly might wish to borrow to finance capital expenditure, just as the local authorities currently do. This has been ruled out by the Constitutional Convention, but warrants consideration, not least in the context of the relationship between regional Assemblies and local authorities, but also because of the development of the Private Finance Initiative. There needs to be some consideration of how an Assembly might finance capital expenditure. These logistical issues and issues of principle in relation to borrowing are considered in Chapter 7.

To conclude, the purpose of this report is not to propose a particular set of financial arrangements for the Assemblies. Rather it is to point out a wide range of issues which need to be addressed before the introduction of legislation. It is thus intended to provide some pointers to the agenda which policy-makers should be following. Our views as to the key elements of this agenda are drawn out in the concluding chapter.

2 Financing Devolution: the background

Introduction

Since the creation of the United Kingdom, there has been continual conflict over the location of political power. The assumption that all key decisions should be made at Westminster has been regularly challenged. Pressure for devolution, particularly in Scotland, has been one of the few constants of British political life. Nevertheless, the Mother of Parliaments has been remarkably resistant to dilution of her powers. Indeed, during the last sixteen years, the tendency has been towards greater centralisation, particularly at the expense of the autonomy of local authorities. As a result, there is a greater concentration of legislative power in Westminster than in almost all other Western democratic parliaments.

Though legislative power is centred in Westminster, much of the *administration* of power has been devolved from London, particularly to Scotland. The Scottish Office administers almost all of the major functions of government. However, the scope for policy *formulation* is necessarily limited. Administrative devolution permits only a very limited freedom to revise policy to take account of local circumstances. In practice, those making revisions to suit Scottish circumstances, say, invariably belong to the majority party in Central Government. Their ability to deviate from the policies set by their Cabinet colleagues, and their enthusiasm for doing so, is necessarily limited by the constraints of party unity.

Thus, the devolution which has occurred since 1707 has been almost exclusively administrative in character. A brief synopsis of the history of devolution from 1707 to 1973 is given in Appendix 1. At no time has there been any significant extension of localised powers to design and implement legislation. The only exception is Northern Ireland, which is discussed in the next section. The Constitutional Convention's reports are clearly influenced by this history of administrative devolution in the sense that their plans for legislative devolution are very much built on the existing structures of administrative devolution. The existence of a wide range of administrative powers in Scottish Office has inevitably influenced the range of legislative powers which the Convention has proposed for Scotland. The absence of an equivalent government department in the English regions is a major practical obstacle to the introduction of legislative devolution in these areas.

The Constitutional Convention's proposal for an Assembly is, however, only one amongst several which have been mooted in recent decades. These encompass a wider range of powers and financing mechanisms and are worth briefly reviewing here both to develop a historical perspective on this debate and to widen the debate on powers and finance. We take these in chronological order, leading up to the proposals of the Scottish Constitutional Convention, but first we review the experience of Northern Ireland – the only part of the UK to have experienced legislative devolution.

Devolution in Northern Ireland

The exception to this pattern of solely administrative devolution in the UK is Northern Ireland, which experienced legislative devolution during the period 1920–72. The failure of the financing mechanism, in particular, has a bearing on current discussions for the rest of the UK.

It was originally intended that the Northern Irish Parliament, set up in 1920, would be temporary until a unified parliament could be set up in conjunction with the Dublin administration. However, the South's rejection of the proposals meant that the Northern Ireland government at Stormont had an unexpectedly long lifespan.

The 1920 Government of Ireland Act set out the division of legislative and financial power between Westminster and Belfast, a general grant of power being issued to allow the Parliament to legislate for peace, order and good government in the province. This power was subject to certain limitations. Westminster retained power over matters where a uniform approach across the UK was deemed appropriate. These included the Crown, the armed forces, foreign affairs and external trade. Westminster also kept the right to levy certain taxes such as income tax, surtax, customs and excise duties, although some taxation powers were assigned to Stormont, the most important being motor vehicle licence duties.

The allocation of tax revenues and expenditures in Northern Ireland were a major problem for Stormont. Originally, it was assigned all revenues raised in the province to pay Westminster an 'Imperial Contribution' to cover the cost of those services retained at Westminster. It was then free to allocate the remainder of its revenues on devolved services as it saw fit. Almost immediately it was apparent that Northern Ireland could not finance a level of service equivalent to that of the rest of the UK from its own revenues. Adjustments to the funding arrangements were made. Eventually the Imperial Contribution became negative – the British exchequer was contributing to the cost of locally provided services and accepting that Northern Ireland could not make any contribution to the costs of services provided by Westminster. In 1938 the financial arrangements of the province changed from being revenue-based to expenditure-based when the Simon Declaration promised that the UK would make good any deficit in Northern Ireland (subject to some conditions), so underwriting public service standards in Northern Ireland.

This was effected through a variety of mechanisms: first, responsibility for agriculture reverted to Westminster, so that agricultural subsidies were paid out of the Westminster budget; second, contributions were made to the National Insurance Fund in Northern Ireland; third, transfers were made to cover most of the additional cost of health and social services arising from greater need. Latterly the formula for calculating Northern Ireland's share of reserved taxes was modified in a favourable direction (based on population share). In the meantime, Northern Ireland expenditure was squeezed, resulting in reduced capital spending on health, education and housing.

The periodic ad hoc adjustments to Northern Ireland's financing arrangements are evidence of the failure of the original plan. This failure stemmed from the requirement for Northern Ireland to balance its budget in spite of the combination of a relatively poor tax base, and relatively high needs. Because of the continued principle of budgetary balance, met only with the assistance of additional transfers from Westminster, London exercised increasing power over Northern Ireland expenditure in areas which had initially been devolved. 'He who pays the piper calls the tune' is a saying which has wide applicability to discussions of devolution and its financing.

Blueprints for Devolution

Nearly all plans for legislative devolution have proposed a financing mechanism based on some form of block grant. Their avoidance of tax assignment schemes possibly reflect its failure in Northern Ireland. But few of these putative schemes have gone into any detail as to how this block grant will be determined. Since the purpose of any funding scheme is to resource a particular range of expenditures, the composition of this range will have a bearing on the success of financing mechanism. Therefore, we now review the proposals for the powers to be devolved to the Assemblies. We pick up the story in 1973, when the Royal Commission on the Constitution published a report which was to be highly influential in all subsequent plans for devolution.

The Royal Commission on the Constitution (1973)

(a) The Commission's Models of Devolution

In the early 1970s, a Royal Commission under Lord Kilbrandon was given the remit of examining constitutional change in the UK. It reported in 1973 on models for devolution in England, Scotland and Wales. These included legislative and executive devolution, the establishment of advisory councils and increased devolution to local authorities, combined with a system of regional committees of representatives from the local authorities.

Under the proposals for *legislative devolution*, a territorial legislature was to be created consisting of the Sovereign and a directly elected Assembly. Although the UK Parliament would retain ultimate legislative authority, the Assembly could legislate on several functions transferred to its control. Control of some functions was to be retained at Westminster, including the supply of electricity and some functions in the field of agriculture, fisheries and food such as price support measures and other grants and subsidies.

By *executive devolution* it was intended that the *framework* of legislation and policy would remain under Central Government control whilst the elected Assembly would have responsibility over subordinate policy making and administration. The Assembly would exercise its responsibility in broadly the same way as local authorities exercise their statutory functions – parliament would lay down policy in broad terms and leave the details to be filled in by the Assembly.

An alternative Kilbrandon proposal – that of an *advisory council*, on the other hand, required no devolution of legislative or executive powers, but rather the creation of a directly elected council with powers to scrutinise Central Government policies and to offer advice to Ministers as to how they might be applied in each territory. The council would be given clearly defined powers to call for information from relevant government offices and to question officials about the administration of policy. The report suggested that it would be given powers to consider: economic and employment problems; nationalised industries; priorities for major road and other developments; land use proposals for such things as mineral prospecting or the siting of defence establishments and the organisation and administration of public services.

These councils were to consist mainly of members of the local authorities in each territory although a minority of members would be nominated by a Minister responsible for regional affairs so as to secure representation from industry and commerce, trade unions and education etc. As many functions as possible would be devolved directly to the local authorities while the advisory councils would provide a means of expressing the overall needs of the region to all levels and agencies of government. One of the most important functions of the council would be to advise on government spending in the region, based on an annual debate. This was envisaged as a means of making the centre aware of any desire for changed territorial priorities.

The final model in the Kilbrandon Report was based on an increase in the power of the local authorities. A formal *arrangement of co-operation was to be made between local authorities*. This scheme was proposed only to apply in England. The proposals for co-ordination were principally concerned with planning activities. It was intended that local authorities submit plans to regional committees before requesting Ministerial approval. Similarly, the House of Commons would create regional committees of its own Members to consider plans for the regions.

(b) The Commission's Findings

The Commissioners who signed the majority report broadly favoured a system of legislative devolution for Scotland. Opinion was divided on the issue of Welsh devolution, with six Commissioners favouring legislative devolution, three preferring a Welsh Assembly with deliberative and advisory functions and the remaining two supporting executive devolution. The Commission was also split in its opinion over which solution was most suitable for England. The majority favoured a system of nonexecutive co-ordinating and advisory councils. The proposed councils would be set up in each of the eight English regions which had been established for the purpose of economic planning. There was some support for executive devolution to directly elected regional Assemblies along the lines of that proposed for Scotland and Wales. Also supported were proposals for maximum devolution to local authorities combined with a system of regional committees of representatives from the local authorities.

(c) The Memorandum of Dissent

A minority of two of the Commissioners, Lord Crowther-Hunt and Professor AT Peacock, proposed a radically different scheme. Their views were published in the form of a memorandum of dissent. Their scheme was to apply in the same form to the whole of the UK. Seven Assemblies were to be elected on the basis of proportional representation – one for Scotland, one for Wales and the remaining five for the English regions.

The key features of this system were that these Assemblies were to have substantial powers over strategic planning, health, water, police, education, housing and general welfare. Thus, its proposals were for a radically different system of government in the UK with a symmetric system of regional Assemblies.

Scottish and Welsh Proposals (1978)

In 1978, the Scotland Act was introduced by the Labour government. Its intention was to create legislative devolution in Scotland. All those powers which were to be devolved and those that were specifically not to be devolved were listed in a Schedule to the Act. The new Scottish institutions were to be responsible for most functions of government within Scotland and were intended to form part of a strengthened democratic process within the UK. Two bodies were to be set up, an Assembly and an Executive, the former being responsible for legislative matters and the latter dealing with the administrative aspects of the devolved powers.

The Assembly and the Executive were to be free to determine expenditure on the devolved services as they saw fit, financing such spending from a block grant allocated to Scotland by the UK Exchequer. This mechanism, although never adopted for funding devolved services, became the model for Central Government's block funding in Scotland, Wales and Northern Ireland subsequently. Further discussion of this mechanism, which was known at the time as the Barnett formula, is postponed until Chapter 4.

The Act allowed for borrowing to meet short-term fluctuations in liquidity. No long-term borrowing powers were to be granted. Capital expenditure was to be met from the Block Grant. Local authorities would, however, continue to be allowed access to the Public Works Board and to financial markets. The implications of such borrowing powers to any future Assembly is discussed more fully in Chapter 7.

The Act set out twenty five groups of powers that were to be devolved to the Scottish institutions, falling under the following broad headings: health, social welfare, education etc., housing, local government & local finance, pollution, the countryside, land use & development, transport, roads etc., erosion & flooding, marine works fisheries, agricultural land, water etc., fire services, courts & the legal profession, tourism, public records, tribunals & inquiries, ancient monuments, crime, registration service, civil law matters, miscellaneous.

The last covered a group of services such as charities, public holidays, licensing and trading regulations. Within each major group of functions, there were further subdivisions, some of which were to be devolved, while others were to remain under the control of Westminster. For example, although primary and secondary education services were to be devolved to the Scottish institutions, matters relating to universities were to remain the remit of Westminster. Similarly, only powers over the physical provision of roads which were to be assigned to the Scottish parliament, the regulation of road users still remaining a national issue.

Those functions retained by Central Government were either intended to maintain the integrity of national economic policy or were justified by the need to maintain consistency of relationships with foreign countries. These included: defence, foreign policy, police, social security and macroeconomic policy.

Thus, the approach adopted for the assignment of powers to the Assembly was highly prescriptive, listing those policies to be devolved and those to be retained centrally. It was not based on any particular principle. This contrasts with the Convention's approach which cites the *principle of subsidiarity* to guide the allocation of power. We deal with this issue in more detail subsequently.

The Scotland and Wales Bill also proposed a directly elected Assembly for Wales but with no power to legislate, unlike its Scottish counterpart. Thus, the Westminster Parliament would continue to legislate on behalf of Wales in devolved matters. Those matters to be devolved were in the main similar to those proposed for Scotland, although the Scottish Assembly's powers were to be slightly more extensive. As in Scotland, the Welsh Assembly would have no remit to consider matters requiring national action. The post of Secretary of State for Wales was to be retained with the function of overseeing non-devolved services in Wales.

The devolved services were to be financed through a Block Grant, with the Assembly having complete discretion over its allocation. The Grant was to be determined on an annual basis through close discussions between the Assembly and the UK government. No explicit method of determining the allocation was suggested. As in Scotland, Welsh taxpayers were to pay UK taxes at UK rates and the revenues from these were to be allocated to a central fund from which the Block Grant and other national expenditure would be drawn.

The Constitutional Convention's Proposals for Scotland

The most comprehensive current proposals for devolution in Scotland are those of the Constitutional Convention. Its report provides the bestavailable blueprint of a devolved Scottish Assembly should the Labour Party be successful at the next election.

The Convention's report suggests that a Scottish Parliament should take over the following functions currently administered by the Scottish Office: education, law, health, local government, training, transport, planning, environment, industry.

The notable difference between these proposals and previous ones is that it is now proposed to apply the principle of subsidiarity to the devolved functions. Rather than providing an extensive list of devolved services, the legislation would lay down a principle requiring decisions to be taken as close as possible to those mainly affected by them. Thus, all matters which affect Scotland alone would fall within the competence of the Scottish administration. For those functions which might be shared between Westminster and Edinburgh, the principle of subsidiarity would be used to determine which level of government should take responsibility.

While such a proposal may seem attractive in principle, its practical application may not be straightforward. For example, suppose that restrictive macroeconomic policy has a tendency to result in higher unemployment in the north of the UK, with little impact elsewhere. The principle of subsidiarity would seem to indicate that because of this differential impact, macroeconomic policy should be devolved – an argument which would surely be unacceptable to Central Government. The interdependence of economic policies controlled by different levels of government means that it is difficult to determine those which are unambiguously affecting particular groups of individuals.

It has also been made explicit that the Scottish Parliament will be responsible for the police force in Scotland and for promoting inward investment and the development of such industries as agriculture, fisheries, forestry and tourism. These are singled out because of their distinct importance to the Scottish economy.

Powers to be explicitly reserved to the Westminster Parliament include matters which, in the Convention's opinion, require co-ordinated action at national level. These include defence, foreign affairs, immigration, social security and macroeconomic policies. Scottish MPs at Westminster would continue to provide a Scottish voice in debates on these matters. The position of Secretary of State for Scotland would also be retained to provide representation for Scotland in the UK Cabinet, although he or she would have no official contact with the Scottish Parliament and thus could not exercise the same control over Scottish affairs.

The Convention proposes that the current system of funding Scottish expenditure through a block grant should be retained. The Scottish Parliament would determine its own spending priorities without Westminster involvement. It would also have the power to vary the standard rate of income tax in Scotland by up to a maximum of 3p in the pound and would have the right to retain revenues generated from increases rates. Any decrease in revenue from cuts in income tax would have be paid from the Block Grant. Chapter 6 addresses the quantitative effects of the exercise of this power.

Conclusion

The history of devolution in Great Britain is that of a gradual and grudging increase in the power of the peripheral areas, particularly Scotland and Wales, to administer legislation formulated by the Westminster government. With the exception of the failed Stormont Parliament, there has been no significant extension of legislative powers to particular parts of the UK since the Act of Union in 1707. Given increased electoral support for some form of legislative devolution of power in recent decades, a number of potential models have been drawn up. The Constitutional Convention argues that the principle of subsidiarity can be applied to determine those powers which should be within the remit of the Assembly. It has already been applied to public administration within Scotland in the sense that most governmental functions in which there is no overriding UK interest are administered through the Scottish Office. However, the subsidiarity principle is not a universal panacea. Because of the interdependence of economic policies, its application is frequently ambiguous. Thus even though there may exist broad political agreement about the powers to be devolved, there are still likely to be opportunities for conflict between the various layers of government. Such possibilities have not been dealt with in any depth in the published reports of the Constitutional Convention. In Chapter 3, we illustrate some of the key issues.

The issue of resourcing the Assemblies has also been given very little attention. the territories of the UK are currently funded by the block grants determined by the Treasury, giving little scope for departure from public spending norms laid down Westminster. Most current proposals for devolution do not envisage significant change from these arrangements, even though this will reduce the effective power of the Assemblies to initiate new policies involving significant additional expenditure. The most radical proposal thus far has been the suggestion by the Constitutional Convention that the Scottish Assembly be given the power to vary the standard rate of income tax by 3p in the pound. This problem of resourcing the powers which the Assemblies might like to exercise is considered in more depth in chapters 4, 5 and 6.

3 Powers of the Assembly

Introduction

The creation of devolved Assemblies will add an extra layer to the structure of government in Britain. If this new structure is to be successful, the relationships between the different layers must be clearly defined. Their powers and the limitations on these powers should be understood both by politicians and by the public. Otherwise, there is a danger of unrealistic expectations leading to crises of confidence in the new structure.

The funding mechanisms should not erode the freedom of each layer to exercise its assigned powers. This freedom is maximised if each layer raises sufficient resources through taxation and borrowing to exercise these powers. It is minimised if all lower layers are dependent on grant funding from, and thus subject to the influence of, higher levels of government. This could arise, for example, if Central Government tried to influence Assembly policy on education by manipulation of the education component of the grant.

Devolution is not a simple choice. There are a multitude of ways in which it might be implemented. Each will result in a different balance of power between central and devolved parliaments. The financial arrangements are as important as the political structures in determining where that balance will lie. This issue forms the main focus of this chapter, but we also consider relationships with other institutions such as industry regulatory bodies and trade unions.

Again, we particularly concentrate on Scotland given that the first Assembly is likely to be established there. To anticipate our conclusions, it is clear that there are several important areas of economic policy where potentially destabilising conflict between the Assembly and other layers of government may occur. To minimise such conflict, the rules of engagement between Assembly and Central Government must be clearly defined in the legislation. Even so, some discord is inevitable.

Service Provision and the Assemblies

As discussed in Chapter 2, the Constitutional Convention has outlined the list of services which it expects to be provided by the Scottish Assembly. These may have been selected through the application of the principle of subsidiarity, though this is not clear from the Convention's reports. They will undoubtedly provide the main focus of activity in the Assembly.

What will happen, however, if Central Government tries to change the list? As already mentioned in Chapter 2, there are now significant political problems in establishing any agreement on the division of services between the public and private sectors. Whatever its merits and demerits, privatisation policy has destroyed the broad consensus on the role of the state which existed in the 1960s and 1970s. Different parties now have quite different views about the composition of the 'public services'.

Once Assemblies are created, it is quite conceivable their majority party will be different from that of Central Government. Due to the centralised nature of the UK tax system, there is little local control over either the collection or distribution of tax revenues. Unlike many Western democracies including Germany and the USA, this centralised fiscal structure implies that UK Central Government largely finances lower levels of government such as local authorities. This gives Westminster a great deal of influence over the services to be provided by lower layers of government. The creation of an Assembly will provide a focus of opposition to that influence.

For example, one might expect a Scottish Assembly to take the view that educational services should be publicly funded, whereas a Conservative Central Government would be quite willing to let private sector educational provision increase. Similarly, Conservatives might argue that water services should be provided by the private sector, whereas a Labour-dominated Scottish Assembly would take the opposite view. More unlikely, but not unthinkable, would be the removal of some medical services from the public sector.

A broad view of individual consumption includes both private sector goods and public sector goods. The effect of privatising some public sector services implies a switch from public to private sector consumption, but it does not necessarily imply a reduction in the level of private expenditure necessary to maintain consumption at its original level. For example, the government could privatise secondary education. So long as there was a legal requirement to attend secondary school, households would experience a drop in their taxes, because of savings in the local authority budget. However, private expenditure would rise since school fees would be demanded from those households with children attending secondary school. The net effect of this change would depend on a number of factors. First, if private sector provision is more efficient than that of the public sector, overall household consumption of both public and private sector goods would increase. Second, there would undoubtedly be distributional effects since, in effect, rich families transfer income to the poor when taxes are used to fund public sector provision.

The transfer of functions from the private to the public sector will not necessarily affect the demand for these services, but it may have efficiency and distributional consequences. The Assembly may have a different view from Westminster about the appropriate form of provision. Suppose that Westminster privatises some service and the Assembly refuses to follow the same path. Westminster may then legitimately argue that the Assembly electorate should not benefit from the tax cuts realised as a result of the privatisation. After all, if the demand for the service is unchanged, households will have to pay for it directly rather than through taxation. This would suggest that tax rates should vary across the UK, depending on territorial provision of public service. This may be tenable, but only to a limited extent. Radically different views between Westminster and other parts of the country with respect to service provision, will undermine the stability of the Assemblies. Again, this reinforces the argument, to which we return in subsequent chapters, for some kind of buffering mechanism which partially obstructs changes in service provision between Westminster and the Assemblies.

Even if Central Government and Assembly can agree on the range of functions to be provided by the public sector, there will still be opportunity for conflict. For those functions involving resource allocation, conflict arises principally because of their interdependence. For example, in recent years macroeconomic policy has tended to move away from Keynesian 'fine tuning' through monetary and fiscal interventions. Instead, supply-side economics which emphasises the need to develop flexible and efficient product and labour markets has come to the fore. This requires microeconomic interventions in areas such as training, research and development, industrial regulation etc. A simplistic application of the principle of subsidiarity might make the Assembly responsible for these functions. If it takes a different view from Central Government on training strategy, conflict is likely. This will arise because different layers of government are prepared to argue that they have a vital and legitimate interest in this area of policy.

Similarly, the report of the Constitutional Convention implies that the Assembly will take an active interest in the health of Scottish industry. For political reasons one might expect it to try to protect 'the Scottish interest' more forcefully than Central Government. For example, it may oppose take-overs of major Scottish firms on the grounds that they weaken Scottish control of Scottish industry. In contrast, Westminster may argue that take-overs promote both efficiency and shareholder returns. The Assembly will almost inevitably become a political focus in debates on such issues. The provision of such a focus is part of the purpose of devolution. But where the extension of devolution is not symmetric across the UK – the ability to provide such a well-defined focus is likely to cause resentment in the rest of the country. Thus, even in those areas of economic policy where Central Government may have primary responsibility, political intervention by the Assembly may lead to strains in the relationships between Central Government and Assembly and between different parts of the UK.

Similarly, use of powers to buy equity stakes in Scottish companies, which is also mentioned by the Constitutional Convention, may conflict with industrial policy in other parts of the UK. If there are to be no provisions for borrowing and, as one would expect, equity purchases are not accommodated within the block grant arrangements, the only possible source of such funding would come from tax variation powers.

One way of increasing resources is to allow the Assemblies latitude to tax or borrow. Taxation has the clear advantage of accountability: the current electorate has to pay for the increase in services for which it has expressed a desire. Borrowing is somewhat more indirect and its impact on current taxpayers will depend on the terms of the loans it incurs. The implications of these issues are discussed more fully in Chapters 5 and 6.

It is impossible to anticipate all possible conflicts over the services and financing of the Assembly. One means of dealing with such arguments would be to create a body with the specific role of arbitrating in disputes between the Assemblies and Central Government. Both parties would make a case to this body based on a set of principles laid down in the legislation and its decision would be binding. Having a third party to resolve conflict between government and Assembly would reduce the intensity of disputes between these bodies and thus stabilise their relationship. A body such as the Australian Commonwealth Grants Commission could possibly act as adjudicator. We discuss this possibility in Chapter 6.

One could argue that changes in resources granted to the Assembly arising purely from variation in macroeconomic circumstances would be given an over-riding priority to which no objection by the Assembly would have any force. On the other hand, sudden reductions in resources due to the imposition by Central Government of a cut in the functions resourced by the public purse would not be permitted. Thus, as argued above, Central Government would not be permitted to cut funding from the Assembly because of a short-run decision that dentistry should be wholly privately funded, for example.

An alternative might be to write into the legislation a clearly specified list of functions to be resourced through the Block Grant. This might comprise items such as education, health, local government etc. The functions could be reviewed on an infrequent basis to provide for new ones to be added and/or existing ones to be withdrawn. This concept of entrenchment would provide greater security to the Assemblies in their formative years and is supported by those political parties actively engaged in debating the issue of devolved Assemblies (Scottish Constitutional Convention 1994). As with the arbitration scheme described above, this mechanism would also prevent the Block Grant being cut, for example, because Central Government decided to privatise dentistry against the wishes of the Assembly.

The way in which such a list of functions is specified is also of importance. Too detailed an approach would stifle diversity where policies of the Assembly and those of Central Government differ; for example, if Central Government decided to support nursery education while the Assembly did not. A loosely specified list could result in regular disputes. There is a danger, which we discuss in Chapter 4, that reliance on the principle of subsidiarity to determine where control of functions should be located will lead to ambiguity, and raise the likelihood of conflict between different layers of government.

Service provision by local government is another potentially thorny issue for the Assembly. It may take the view that the role of local government is to provide a particular group of services or to enable their provision by the private sector. The Assemblies will be relatively new political institutions and will understandably wish to cast themselves in a favourable light with their electorate. Where the Assembly controls local authority allocations, there will be a temptation to reduce the autonomy of local authorities by resourcing them to provide a very specific set of services. This exactly mirrors the argument concerning the relationship between Central Government and Assemblies. Similar conflicts may arise and again some kind of safeguards may require to be built into the legislation to preserve the autonomy of local government. Within this framework, there is also potential for strategic alliances between central and local government to undermine the authority of the Assemblies. Again some insitutionalised mechanism system of checks and balances is required to minimise this risk.

To conclude, harmonious relationships between all three layers of government are contingent on a clear understanding of the services to the public which each is to provide and an adequate resourcing of these. Without some form of protection for lower level authorities, the higher levels may seek to exploit their power over resource allocation to dictate the type and form of service provision which the lower levels should make. If there is no revenue sharing between layers of government, then protection of lower levels will require not only careful framing of the legislation setting up the Assemblies but also some independent third party to arbitrate in disputes.

The Assembly as Regulator

Different layers of government also have a number of regulatory roles. These include awarding contracts to private sector service suppliers and checking compliance with these contracts. Examples of such services might include refuse collection, prisons and school meals. Regulation of industry on public interest issues such as health and safety is also seen as a legitimate role of government. Potential market failure motivates regulation of industries where significant monopoly power exists. Finally, upper layers of government may take powers to regulate the activities of lower levels. For example, Central Government in the UK, through bodies such as the Audit Commission, monitors the efficiency of service delivery by local authorities. Here we discuss some specific examples of such issues which require to be given consideration in setting up the Assemblies.

Several major Scottish industries are regulated by UK bodies. Most firms in these industries previously belonged to the nationalised sector. These include Scottish Power, Hydro-Electric and Scottish Nuclear. Similar firms have a major impact on the Scottish economy, but cannot be described as Scottish-based. British Gas and British Telecom, for example, are both major suppliers of services to Scottish customers and large local employers.

The position of one industry is particularly anomalous: the water industry is privatised in England and Wales, and regulated by OFWAT. In Scotland, this industry has remained within the public sector, and is regulated by the Secretary of State. OFWAT has no remit within Scotland.

A Scottish Assembly might have an interest in the activities of such utilities for a variety of reasons. First, consumers might put pressure on Assembly members to reduce prices and to improve quality of service, just as they currently do with Westminster MPs. Second, employees could plead their case with the Assembly should some unwelcome change in working conditions be proposed. Third, the companies themselves might lobby the Assembly for support against competition from elsewhere or for assistance with investment programmes etc.

The Assembly could be given the power to regulate all of these industries in Scotland. This would lead to a number of difficulties. For example, suppose that British Telecom asked for a greater than normal price rise because of some large investment planned in England. It would find little support from a Scottish-based regulator. On the other hand, similar expansion plans by Scottish Power and Hydro-Electric might receive a more sympathetic reception. The pattern of ownership of these industries, the degree of local monopoly power and the level of local employment are all likely to influence the attitude of the Assembly. This is likely to cause deep concern to industries wishing to protect their commercial freedom. Until such suspicions are allayed, it is perhaps appropriate that the Assembly be prevented from playing a role in industry regulation.

Higher levels of government scrutinise the activities of lower levels. They try to ensure that public resources are used effectively and efficiently at lower levels. Bodies such as the Public Accounts Committee and the Audit Commission have been set up with this concept in mind. The former has responsibility for the Value for Money (VFM) initiative. There are three concepts central to the initiative: economy (limitation of inputs); efficiency (mapping the ratio of inputs to outputs); and effectiveness (meeting the objectives). As part of this process a high profile has been given to the development of Performance Indicators (PIs). These PIs allow comparisons to be made between authorities and with the private sector to ensure that the effectiveness of the VFM initiative. The Accounts Committee has a statutory duty to promote such comparative studies designed to enable it to make recommendations for improving VFM in the provision of local services.

A role for such regulatory bodies must surely exist within the structure of the devolved administrations. But this implies very close scrutiny by the Assembly of the activities of local government. This seems to contradict the Scottish Constitutional Convention's view that there should be '*a culture of co-operation at the heart of the relationship between the Parliament and local authorities*' (Scottish Constitutional Convention, 1995). This goes back to the view that the Assembly takes of local government. If it imposes a regime (and it may have little option if it is under pressure from Central Government) which relies heavily on performance indicators and efficiency measures, then through its regulatory role with local authorities, it will effectively force them to concentrate on service provision. The latitude for independent initiative at local level will be blocked.

This will not be welcomed by local authorities who might perhaps expect an Assembly to allow them more scope for independent action. As with the relationship between Central Government and the Assembly, the Assembly's control of the financing of local authorities implies influence over the functions they carry out. This is not particularly healthy for local democracy. If the

Assembly is to allow for differences in the provision of public services as between, say, Shetland and Glasgow, it will have to determine a flexible system of resource allocation which makes this possible.

Conclusions

(1)   The provision of financial resources inevitably will be predicated on Assemblies being responsible for a particular range of services. Yet there is scope for conflict between Westminster and the Assemblies over what services should be provided; the purpose of devolution after all is to provide a mechanism for different regional preferences to be expressed. In matters of dispute, one possibility would be to introduce a statutory delay before changes could be implemented. The Constitutional Convention has suggested arbitration by existing government bodies. It might however be preferable for a body to be set up specifically with the power to intervene in disputes between the Assemblies and Central Government.

(2)   Assemblies might want to have regulatory powers over the sectors under their jurisdiction. Regional regulation would make more sense in some cases than others. But, particularly when devolution is extended to other regions, the ensuing regulatory patchwork could become unworkable. On balance therefore it might be preferable to have a simple principle, that policies to regulate industry should be determined at UK level; regulation should be carried out with respect to the UK as a whole and not just Scotland. Nevertheless, for those cases (such as the financial sector) where the Assembly would have particular regional interests, the alternative to the power of regulation as such would be to have a formal mechanism by which representations from the Assembly could be taken into account when UK regulation is under discussion.

(3)   The same issues of potential conflict between levels of jurisdiction apply equally to the Assembly and the local authorities. If the Assembly wishes to promote local democracy, the implication is that the Assembly would need to allow local authorities greater freedom to determine their own policies by adopting a more flexible approach to funding.

4 The Barnett Formula

Introduction

In this chapter we consider the main mechanism by which government finance is allocated between the territories of England, Wales, Scotland and Northern Ireland – the Block. Though the current Block is an internal allocation device for distributing resources to the territories, it is being proposed as a model for resource transfer to the Assemblies. In contrast to the current system, these transfers will be external – between central and regional government – with a distinct possibility that these governments will be controlled by different political parties.

It is through the Block that the bulk of the major government services in Scotland – *health, education, transport and local government* – are currently resourced. Its value is largely determined by negotiation between the Treasury and the major spending departments in England and Wales – the Department of Health, Department of the Environment etc. rather than through direct negotiation between Treasury and Scottish Office.

In practice, the Scottish Office has little control over the size of the Block due to the way it is set. Thus, as noted in the previous chapter, its latitude for independent action is tightly constrained. The present method for determining the Block has a history stretching back to the last century. The current formula, in use since its conception at the time of the last devolution debates in the 1970s, was designed to bring about convergence in territorial spending – i.e. equal per capita expenditure. But its operation during the 1980s has proved that, despite expectations, it offers no firm guarantee of any form of equalisation of resources between the territories. In this chapter we review these issues as they impinge on the design of financing arrangements for devolution.

Not all government expenditure is included in the Block. Some categories of spending have moved between components of the Block; some expenditures which might be considered as part of the Block seem somehow to bypass the formula. We discuss whether these exceptions are important and the difficulties they might cause an elected Scottish Assembly. Finally, we consider the political economy of the Block Grant – its credibility, sustainability and, ultimately, its prospect for political longevity.

Historical Background

Most public expenditure in Scotland originates from a Block which is determined in the pre-budget allocation to government departments. The size of this allocation varies in line with the government's overall spending strategy. If it decides to cut expenditure to meet its macroeconomic objectives, resources to Scotland will be reduced broadly in line with the cuts applied to the rest of the UK. Thus, as noted in the previous chapter, macroeconomic considerations are the principal determinants of total public resources allocated to Scotland, as they are to the rest of the UK.

Once English spending (or British, in the case of the Northern Ireland Block) is known, allocation to Scotland, Wales and Northern Ireland is largely determined by a formula, currently known as the *Barnett Formula*, but whose origins can be traced back to the Victorian Chancellor of the Exchequer, *George Goschen*. He created a formula which allocated public spending in the ratio: Scotland 11 per cent; Ireland 9 per cent; and England and Wales the remaining 80 per cent of all UK spending. The basis for these shares is disputed, argued to be either the territories' share of the British population based on the 1881 census or derived from overall contributions of probate duties to the Exchequer (Mitchell 1991). Its use is equally difficult to track since it was not universally applied to territorial services. It was, however, in use until 1959, principally in relation to education spending through the period 1918 to 1959.

In the following two decades, financial allocation to the Scottish Office operated in an ad hoc fashion; no formula being regularly applied. Then, in 1978, when the devolution debate focused attention on public expenditure in England, Scotland and Wales, Labour's Chief Secretary to the Treasury, *Joel Barnett*, produced a new formula. Since then, his name has been associated with this essentially revised and updated version of the discarded Goschen formula. Although the aims of the two formulae were different, the underlying concept of a population base for allocating resources was common to both. For the first time Welsh expenditure appeared as a separate entity rather than in conjunction with English programmes. The formula, based on 1976 population figures, allocated Scotland £10 and Wales £5 for every £85 *change* in expenditure on comparable English service programmes. This amounted to Scotland receiving 11.76 per cent of any change in English expenditure and Wales 5.88 per cent. A parallel formula, *Son-of-Barnett*, was applied to Northern Ireland's expenditure needs. By this means Northern Ireland received 2.75 per cent of any change in equivalent expenditure on services in Great Britain.

The formula remained untouched until 1992 when it was revised by the Chief Secretary to the Treasury, *Michael Portillo*, to reflect Scotland's declining share of the UK population. Portillo cut Scotland's share back to 10.66 per cent of changes in comparable English expenditure and 10.06 per cent of changes in combined English and Welsh programmes such as Law and Order. Wales was to receive 6.02 per cent of any change in English expenditure and Northern Ireland 2.87 per cent of changes in British expenditure. The change was accompanied by promises by the Scottish Secretary of State that the recalibrated Barnett formula would not produce a reduction in Scotland's public expenditure relative below that justified on the basis of relative needs. We take up the issue of what is meant by relative need in Chapter 6.

The Barnett Formula in Practice

Here we consider how the Barnett formula presently operates. We begin by illustrating how the Scottish Office Block is set. Suppose that there are only two components in government spending – health and local authorities. Current expenditure on these in England is, say, £34bn and £30bn. Suppose that for political reasons the Chancellor decides to freeze health expenditure and increase local authority resources by 10 per cent to £33bn. As a result, applying the Portillo factor of 10.66 per cent, the overall increase in the Scottish Office budget would be £320m and would stem solely from the increase in local authority spending. If, in contrast, the decision had been made to freeze local authority resources and increase English health spending by 10 per cent, the increase in the Scottish Office budget would be £362m. Thus, changes in the resources which Scotland receives are dependent on the distribution of changes between spending departments in England and ultimately on the political decisions which determine this distribution.

Overall, the resources allocated through the Barnett formula depend on relative levels of spending when it was introduced and on the relative change in expenditure during the time the formula has operated. As the above example illustrates it is applied only to *changes* in expenditure. In Northern Ireland, Son-of-Barnett operates in much the same way. By operating only on changes in spending, it was intended that the formula would gradually result in convergence of per capita spending in the territories. When it was introduced, there were noticeable differences in the expenditure of the territories relative to population. The formula was intended to ensure that these differences would be eliminated as is explained in the following example.

Table 1 shows how changes in public expenditure alter the ability of the formula to achieve the convergence in per capita levels of expenditure. Though the figures are entirely hypothetical, they accurately represent the effects of the formula under different assumptions about growth in public spending. Initially, Scotland has higher per capita public expenditure than England: it receives one eighth of the expenditure but has only one tenth of the population. The table then shows how per capita expenditure in England and Scotland changes after the Barnett formula has been applied under three different assumptions about overall growth in public spending. No change in population takes place between Year 1 and Year 2.

The percentage increases in per capita spending shown in the final column shows that convergence (or divergence) of per capita expenditure is dependent on the rate at which government expenditure is changing. In Case 1, public expenditure in Great Britain increases by 20 per cent. This overall increase is then allocated by applying the formula in the ratio 90:10 to England and Scotland respectively. This means that Scotland receives 11 per cent of any change which takes place in England. The new spending totals are shown in

Table 1: The Barnett Formula and Convergence in Per Capita Expenditure

Territory	Population (Million)	Year 1 Expenditure (£bn)	Per Capita Expenditure (£)	Year 2 Expenditure (£bn)	Per Capita Expenditure (£)	Per Cent Increase
Case 1:	**20 Per Cent Increase in Public Expenditure**					
England	50	175	3,500	211	4,220	20.6%
Scotland	5	25	5,000	29	5,800	16.0%
Great Britain	55	200	3,636	240	4,364	20.0%
Case 2:	**0 Per Cent Increase in Public Expenditure**					
England	50	175	3,500	175	350	00.0%
Scotland	5	25	5,000	25	5,000	0.0%
Great Britain	55	200	3,636	200	3,636	0.0%
Case 3:	**10 Per Cent Decrease in Public Expenditure**					
England	50	175	3,500	157	3,140	−10.3%
Scotland	5	25	5,000	23	4,600	−8.0%
Great Britain	55	200	3,636	180	3,273	−10.0%

the fourth column. The fifth column shows the level of per capita expenditure in the second year in England and Scotland. The final column shows that per capita spending in England has grown by 20.6 per cent between Year 1 and Year 2, while that in Scotland has only grown by 16 per cent. Thus, in this example, per capita spending in England is catching up on that in Scotland. This convergence is fastest when expenditure is increasing rapidly. When public spending is not growing at all, as in Case 2, there is no change to allocate to territories and therefore no convergence. Finally, in Case 3, when spending is decreasing, divergence occurs with the gap between per capita spending in England and that in Scotland increasing.

Thus, while in theory the Barnett formula should achieve convergence in per capita expenditure in the territories, in practice the rate of this convergence is subject to the overall rate at which government expenditure is changing. In turn, this is dependent on the rate of inflation, the real rate of growth and the share of public spending in GDP. As in recent times, low inflation and continuing pressure to reduce real public expenditure produces very slow convergence. This is one of the key arguments which explains why Scotland's public spending per head in areas such as health, education and local government continues to exceeds that in England by a considerable margin.

Achieving speedy convergence of per capita expenditure in the territories is not the prime interest of the Chancellor when determining the level of public spending. Macroeconomic and policy-related issues take precedence. If territorial equalisation was a primary objective of the Treasury, then it would not rely on the Barnett formula, which is rather a blunt instrument to achieve this objective.

We can also show the results of applying a Barnett-type formula with a more formal approach. For the moment setting aside the issue of population change, the variable in which we are interested is the rate of change in relative public expenditure between Scotland and England. Let the levels of expenditure in these territories be x_E and x_S respectively and let t denote time. This relative rate of change, after some manipulation, can be expressed as shown in the right hand side of (1). See Appendix (2) for some further details:

$$\frac{\partial\left(\frac{x_E}{x_E}\right)}{\partial t} = \frac{1}{x_E}\frac{\partial x_S}{\partial x_E}\frac{\partial x_E}{\partial t} - \frac{x_S}{x_E^2}\frac{\partial x_E}{\partial t} \tag{1}$$

The relative change of expenditure (not the rate of change) in the two areas, $\partial x_S/\partial x_E$ is governed by the Goschen, Barnett or Portillo factor, φ. Thus (1) can be rewritten as:

$$\frac{\partial\left(\frac{x_S}{x_E}\right)}{\partial t} = \left(\varphi - x_X\frac{S}{x_E}\right)\frac{1}{x_E}\frac{\partial x_E}{\partial t} = \left(\varphi - \frac{x_S}{x_E}\right)\frac{\partial \ln x_E}{\partial t} \tag{2}$$

This equation has a simple interpretation. It shows that the rate of change in relative expenditure between Scotland and England depends on the overall growth rate in public spending in England and on the difference between the current expenditure shares and their target ratio φ. It is obvious that relative expenditure shares will not change if there is no growth in public expenditure in England. Further, once the relative shares are equal to their target value, φ, then no further change will take place, whatever the rate of growth in public spending. Lastly, if the initial expenditure shares exceed the target set by the Barnett formula (φ $<x_S/x_E$), the rate of change of relative expenditure shares will be negative. With the reverse effect occurring when expenditure shares are less than the Barnett factor, the system will tend to stabilise around φ. Thus whatever the initial allocations, so long as there is some change in aggregate expenditure, spending by territory will eventually converge to the Barnett shares. However, this is taking considerably longer than the 1970s policymakers originally anticipated.

Scotland has in fact benefited from the retrenchment of public spending in those areas of spending covered by the Block. This can be predicted from equation (2) and from Case 3 in Table 1. Those territories, such as Scotland, with higher per capita spending actually increase their relative advantage when public spending is being cut.

A further factor influencing per capita spending in the territories is population change. The Barnett formula does not take account of population shifts. Rather than have its spending share reduced as intended, Scotland's relative advantage in per capita spending continued to grow during the 1980s because Scotland's population declined relative to the rest of the UK. If the Barnett factor, 10.66 per cent after Michael Portillo's recent amendment and equivalent to φ in Equation 2, is not adjusted to take account of relative changes in population, those territories with declining population will continue to enjoy a relative advantage in per capita spending. This suggests that any block grant based system requires a mechanism for revision in the light of population changes. In practice, this should take account both of current and future population levels in the territories. Current spending would be related to present levels of population, while the factor for capital expenditure, which is incurred for the benefit of both existing and future generations should in addition take account of future population trends..

Official population projections suggest this trend will continue with the Scottish population falling by 4.6 per cent between its 1974 peak and 2,031 compared with a 12 per cent growth in the combined English and Welsh population (Central Statistical Office 1995). If Assembly finance is determined by a form of Barnett formula some adjustment for population shifts would have to be included in the formula. Some agreed form of regular updating of the population base will be required. Failing to account for such change also provides a catalyst for political conflict.

Updating of the population base would also be necessary for other forms of finance. For example, a needs-based approach might conclude that Scottish per capita needs were 10 per cent higher than those in England and Wales. In order to arrive at the total block grant for the Assembly, however, the appropriate per capita grant would have to be grossed up by total population. Again, given the likelihood that Westminster and Edinburgh are controlled by different governments, there will be pressure for the use of accurate population figures so that the level of grant is appropriate.

Formula Bypass

Not all expenditure on areas covered by the Block is actually allocated through the Barnett formula. Occasionally exceptions are made. Thus, the amounts vary from year to year. The importance of this mechanism is not so much in the amount of bypass but rather in its existence. A block grant where there is no latitude for unforeseen contingencies will lead to severe political strain on the relationship between Assembly and Westminster.

The five channels where formula bypass has been identified (Heald 1994) are:

1. Additional expenditure allocations are fixed, not according to the formula, but by costed amounts – e.g. pay awards to NHS staff, if channelled through the Barnett formula would lead to underfunding in areas where numbers of such staff exceeded the average for England and Wales. Such difficulties are circumvented by payments outwith the formula;

2. Local authority outturn expenditure has reflected behavioural patterns not necessarily uniform across all territories affected by the formula; under these circumstances, it would have been expected that overspending in one year would be recouped, if not immediately, at least in the next year, at the expense of other Block services;

3. Certain expenditure functions in the Scottish and Welsh Blocks may have no equivalent in England because services have been terminated or privatised – e.g. the privatisation of the Regional Water Authorities in England and Wales eliminated the comparators for water and sewerage expenditure in Scotland;

4. Certain expenditure changes are allocated on bases other than the Barnett formula, due to changes in macroeconomic policy – e.g. when a package of construction-related work to stimulate the economy was announced in the 1992 Autumn Statement, this expenditure was not issued through the formula but was allocated between the countries such that it would achieve comparable per capita net benefit across the territories;

5. The simple mathematical formulation of the Barnett formula does not address the issue of the mechanics of the Public Expenditure Survey (PES). Each year the Treasury must generate a new horizon year for the purpose of the PES. The first year of last year's PES then becomes the estimated outturn year of the new PAS. Years 2 and 3 of last year's PES then become years 1 and 2 of this year's PES and an entirely new year 3 of

this year's PES is created. Rather than applying the Barnett factor to the Scottish block for year 2, a constant uplift of 2.5% is applied to all PES programmes. This application of an across the board percentage increase implies no change in territorial relatives. Further, when inflation is low and accompanied by low growth of cash expenditure on equivalent English services, a significant part of the increase in block expenditure will stem from this uplift procedure rather than from formula consequences. Such proportional uplifts are more advantageous to the territories than the channelling of funds through the Barnett or Son-of-Barnett formula.

If no bypass flexibility is available and there are no alternative sources of funding, the devolved parliaments may find themselves in funding difficulties which can only be circumvented by borrowing or taxation. Those provisions which are currently made through the process of formula bypass do not produce any serious long term deviations since they largely constitute one-off payments which are then taken account of in future years. For example, a pay rise to nurses may initially be funded through bypass but thereafter it could be consolidated into the Block Grant.

Allocating funds to the territories outside the formula may be acceptable at present, while the formula still applies to an internal allocation mechanism, but if the formula is to be adopted as the means of transferring resources to the devolved administrations, then the issue of bypass would need to be made more transparent. A solution needs to be found whereby in special circumstances payments for services can still be made outwith any formula, even in areas in which power has been devolved to the Assemblies. It would be undesirable for the Assembly necessarily to have to cut other services in order to find the extra finance needed to meet special demands. An alternative to this would be to allow the Assemblies independent taxation powers. Further discussion of this appears in Chapter 6. A second possibility would be to allow borrowing powers, as discussed in Chapter 7.

A further issue concerns those programmes which are not, nor were intended to be, included in the present Scottish Block. The Block covers only approximately 95 per cent of expenditure within the Secretary of State for Scotland's responsibility. Spending on agriculture, fisheries and food and the nationalised industries is not calculated by the formula method. Agricultural expenditure is determined on a Great Britain basis. Further, funding does not come solely from the UK Exchequer; some 67 per cent of agricultural spending in Scotland, mainly for market support and structural measures, comes from EU receipts. Those few remaining nationalised industries are financed on an individual basis.

The Scottish Constitutional Convention proposes that responsibility for agriculture in Scotland be transferred to the Assembly. It follows that agriculture expenditure should be included if a Block Grant is the chosen financing mechanism. However, Scottish farming forms a much higher proportion of British farming than does the Scottish population of the British population.

Applying a population-based formula to such spending would not provide an adequate service provision in Scotland where relative needs are above the UK population proportion. This is essentially why Scottish agriculture remains outside the Block. There is no logic in trying to include such expenditure within a Block Grant formula unless it takes account of Scotland's share of different types of farming.

For example, suppose that the powers of the Assembly include fisheries protection. The Block Grant will therefore be expected to cover the costs of such protection. The notion of equal per capita public spending which underlies the Block Grant approach, implies 'spending' by each individual on fisheries protection is the same, no matter where they are located in the UK. But Scotland, because of its long coastline and active fishery, has a much larger share of fisheries protection activity than its population share might suggest. If per capita spending is equalised, as implied by a Block Grant approach, Scotland would not be able to sustain the same level of protection as that around England and Wales without cross-subsidising fisheries protection from some other spending programme.

The Political Economy of the Block Grant

The Barnett formula was not intended to address differences in the per capita needs of the territories. The formula has been used for a defined set of services for which relative need was considered fairly stable over time and proxied by relative population. Only in the case of some of the examples of formula bypass above has the issue of territorial relative need been addressed. One significant failing of the formula has been the lack of transparency regarding comparable expenditure between the territories. Definitions of English equivalent expenditure have never been published for the two Blocks (Scotland and Wales) nor British comparable expenditure as relates to the Northern Ireland Block. Either the Treasury does not consider territorial expenditure an important issue or the territorial departments want to avoid provoking disputes with the English spending departments.

The most notable difference between the allocation process in England and that in Scotland (Wales) is the absence of bargaining over expenditure cuts/increases between the Treasury and the Scottish (Welsh) Secretary of State. All the negotiation lies with the determination of English expenditure on comparable services. Once each of the English Ministers has argued for his share and been allocated a proportion of public expenditure, the Scottish (Welsh) Secretary is granted a Block consisting of 10.66 per cent (6.02 per cent) of the changes agreed for all of the comparable English services. Thus the expenditure parameters for Scotland and Wales are determined by a procedure unconnected with any political debate over Scottish or Welsh policies. Only spending outwith the Block requires direct consultation between the Secretary of State and the Treasury.

Paradoxically, there are advantages in having expenditure allocated on the basis of a formula derived from the spending priorities of another territory. Some argue that the Barnett formula makes Scotland and Wales dependent on decision-making with respect to England and are denied the use of their own initiative. However, this asymmetry in the Block system allows the Secretary of State to determine his own expenditure priorities within the Block, free from Treasury intervention. If this right is not exercised in full it is a matter of choice, probably reflecting priorities which are likely to be similar to those of the rest of the Cabinet. The politically-sensitive question of territorial expenditure is rarely raised at UK level, except for occasions when the formula is under consideration. Hence the Secretary of State need not normally defend his budget from annual Treasury attacks. Thus Scotland's Block expenditure relative was protected by the Barnett formula at a time when Scotland was suffering diminished political influence in the UK.

The use of a retrospective formula-based allocation mechanism is inflexible in that it does not readily respond to specific changes in the circumstances of the territories. Those who benefit from this inflexibility will seek to defend it and to resist changes in the formula. To the Treasury, the current formula has the advantage of being simple and controllable, leaving no open-ended commitment to spending.

Redefinition of the Planning Total in 1990 had profound implications for the operation of the Barnett formula. Prior to 1990 the Planning Total included Central Government's own expenditure, some expenditure of public corporations, local authority current and capital expenditure (net of receipts), external financing of the nationalised industries, privatisation proceeds and the reserve. After 1990 local authority expenditure was removed and replaced by *Central Government support to local authorities*, defined to include the revenue support grant, non-domestic rates, specific grants and credit approvals (capital allocations in Scotland). External financing of the nationalised industries was also deleted.

As a consequence, the Barnett formula has since applied to a redefined Block within the territorial programmes which must comply with the Treasury's new definitions. By excluding local authority expenditure it was assumed that the formula would apply to a much reduced expenditure base. But the overall effect of the revision has turned out to be smaller than first envisaged, partly due to the treatment of the assigned uniform business rate within *Central Government support to local authorities* and also to the switch of emphasis from *local authority expenditure **excluding** debt interest* to *local authority expenditure **including** debt interest*. Lack of published data relating to equivalent English expenditure on either planning total prohibits judgement on the consequences of the redefinition for block expenditure relatives. However, the relatives will be affected if differentials on Central Government support for local authorities are higher than those on expenditure.

The redefinition of the planning total also affects the way in which the consequences of the Barnett formula can be analysed. The formula is applied to an implied (but not calculated) expenditure aggregate, defined within the planning total . But since 1989 identifiable government expenditure data has been presented in relation to General Government

Expenditure. No reconciliation between the two data sets is published and so the task of comparing identifiable government expenditure and Block expenditure is somewhat opaque.

It can be argued that a mechanism should be provided to protect the composition of the Block after the Assemblies are set up. By this it is meant that some provision should be made about who is to adjudicate on proposals to alter the content of the Blocks. As an example, the 1990 redefinition of the Planning Total affected the size of the Scottish Block. At that time the difference was not of any great significance but it should not be assumed that any future redefinitions would also have a negligible effect.

Conclusion

The Constitutional Convention has proposed a Block Grant system for financing the Scottish Assembly. We would argue that there are a number of potentially serious flaws with this approach, namely:

(1) the way in which the Barnett formula currently operates will eventually lead to equal per capita expenditure in the territories (though as has been demonstrated, the rate of convergence can be slow). This is not necessarily appropriate since it takes no account of variations in need across different parts of the country, nor in differences in the cost of delivery of services.

(2) in particular, there are many areas of public expenditure where a per capita allocation does not seem appropriate. Obvious examples in the Scottish case are fishing and farming, whose activities account for a far larger share of the UK total than a simple population relative would suggest. A more appropriate system would be likely to take account of relative need by moving away from a population based grant system.

(3) if a rigid Block Grant system is introduced and neither borrowing nor taxation powers are available, there will be no flexibility such as the current bypass arrangements to deal with unforeseen contingencies. Even if taxation is available, it will not generate revenues sufficiently quickly to deal with very short-run eventualities

If a decision is taken to move towards a needs-based approach, it is nevertheless likely that the existing mechanisms to determine funding through the Block will be retained during the transitional period. This is partly because it will take some time to conduct the necessary research to complete a needs-assessment. Even in the short-run continuation of a Block system will require a mechanism to deal with unforeseen contingencies. Bypass arrangements have been acceptable because they are intra-government transfers. With greater demands for transparency in financial dealings between Westminster and the Assemblies, formula bypass will almost certainly be impossible as soon as the Assembly is established. A short-term borrowing facility, or an arrangement to bring forward a share of the Block Grant from future allocations up to a set limit, are possible alternatives for dealing with this problem.

If either a needs-assessment or block grant is introduced which requires substantial relative cuts in funding in one or more of the territories, there is a strong argument for phasing in its full effects. One possible method of doing this is to hold back the rate of growth of public expenditure in these territories during periods of rapid growth (above 2.5 per cent, say), while allowing it to increase at the same rate as the rest of the country during recessions. This method of transition would smooth the level of demand in the labour market and hopefully avoid substantial increases in unemployment in the affected territories.

Finally, and perhaps most importantly, a mechanism has to be determined which will allow Westminster and the Assemblies to agree on the range of services which the Block Grant (or needs assessment) is to finance. In Chapter 5 we argue that collection and distribution of tax revenue is not necessarily the exclusive preserve of Central Government. Nevertheless, centralisation is a characteristic of the present system in the UK and it confers on Westminster substantial power to determine the spending priorities of lower level authorities. If Central Government and Assemblies differ in their view of what set of public services should be provided, Westminster can try to impose its will by suitable manipulation of Assembly finance. Such variation will be made easier if the principle of subsidiarity is used to define the location of service provision. Its openness to reinterpretation, particularly in the area of economic policy, will allow Central Government more latitude to change the list of services provided by the Assembly. In contrast, a clear schedule of the services to be provided by both Assembly and Central Government, as used in the 1978 Act, is less ambiguous.

However, future Westminster governments might wish to change this list of services for political or economic reasons by amending the Act setting up the Assembly. To insulate the Assembly from the imposition of unwanted changes in the services it provides, some mechanism will be required which commits both parties to an agreed range of services. The Act itself might specify a mechanism by which changes in the functions of the Assembly could be brought about. For example, this might require a two year delay if both parties agree to the change and a five-year delay (and thus at least one election to both bodies) if no agreement is possible. In practice, this would mean that if Westminster wanted to force water privatisation on an unwilling Scottish Assembly, it would have to wait five years and have this policy survive an election before it could be imposed.

5 Tax Finance

Introduction

An alternative to full block grant funding is to have all or part of Assembly funding explicitly related to tax revenues. This would, at least in principle, create a more transparent connection between revenue and spending in the Assembly and increase its accountability to the electorate. In the 1980s, this was the justification used by the Conservatives for the switch from domestic rates to the community charge – to increase local authority accountability. However, it is unlikely that such assignment would meet the demand for public services in each territory without some form of equalisation grant. We discuss the approximate size of such grants for one specific form of assignment for the fiscal year 1993/94. Finally, the Assemblies could be given separate tax-raising powers. One possible model has been suggested by the Constitutional Convention which would allow a variation of up to 3p in the pound on the standard rate of income tax. We discuss issues related to this power towards the end of this chapter. This chapter considers this and other issues raised by tax-based funding.

Assigning Tax Revenues to the Assembly

If one could start from a blank sheet as far as Assembly financing was concerned, a wide range of alternatives would be available. Here we concentrate on tax assignment. There are two main forms of this financing mechanism. In the first, an agreed proportion of tax revenues raised in a territory is assigned from the central to the territorial authority. Thus, for example, one might assign 50 per cent of all vehicle license duties raised in Scotland to the Assembly. The tax is fully assigned if this proportion is set at 100 per cent. Any other allocation is described as tax sharing.

The second common definition of tax assignment should more accurately be defined as revenue sharing: a proportion of national tax revenue is distributed to each authority, but without regard to the tax yield of the area. For example, allocating to the Scottish Assembly 10 per cent of all vehicle license duty raised in the UK is a revenue sharing mechanism. Both forms of assignment are intended to increase the local accountability of the Assembly and to reduce the influence of Central Government on its spending plans. Germany uses a mixture of both forms of assignment, as the following example demonstrates.

Tax Assignment in Germany

In the system of tax assignment which operates in Germany, neither the Federal Government nor the Lander have exclusive control over the major sources of tax revenue. The German Constitution guarantees that these sources be shared between the two layers of government. That said, some taxes are specifically allocated to a particular level of government whilst others accrue to both levels. A proportion of income taxes is returned to the Lander, the proportion being decided on the basis of the money raised from the tax in each of the Lander. The allocation of revenues cannot be changed without prior alteration of the Constitution. This has the advantage of securing revenues for each Land but has the disadvantage of making it difficult to respond to changes in relative spending needs with changes in income tax shares.

Since 1970, VAT revenues have also been shared between the federal government and the Lander. The VAT share should be considered a revenue-sharing grant rather than tax sharing since the allocation is not determined in accordance with the tax yield in each Land but rather 75 per cent of the yield is distributed amongst the Lander in proportion to their populations and the remaining 25 per cent is used to strengthen the position of Lander whose per capita tax yields are low. VAT returns are distributed in such a manner as to ensure that neither level of government is forced to finance its expenditure by borrowing to a much higher degree than the other.

Compared to tax assignment, revenue sharing favours areas where tax receipts are relatively low. Thus, for example, Scotland would tend to benefit from revenue sharing of income tax based on population shares because estimates of income tax receipts suggest that Scotland's share of these revenues is less than its population share. Thus revenue sharing is a more effective tool for redistributing resources to poorer areas than is tax assignment.

Another substantive difference between revenue sharing and tax assignment relates to national and regional business cycles. Total tax revenues rise and fall with the national business cycle. With revenue sharing, each territory's revenues would move in harmony with this national cycle. However, superimposed on the national business cycle are effects from regional cycles. For example, in the late 1980s, the South-East of England experienced a substantially greater rise in economic activity than other parts of the UK. Conversely, in the early 1990s, the recession in the South-East was more extreme than elsewhere. With tax assignment, its revenues would have first risen and then fallen relatively more than those in the rest of the country. Thus, with tax assignment, Assembly revenues will be more variable in those regions which experience significant regional cycles relative to the rest of the country. This will tend to exaggerate the cycles in such regions. Revenues will be lower during recessions, reducing the freedom of the authorities to offset the reduction in private sector demand with increased demand from the public sector.

Either form of assigned taxation suffers the difficulty that total revenue is still determined by the fiscal stance of Central Government. Budgetary changes in tax rates or in the tax base could substantially affect Assembly revenues. In principle this might seem no different from the uncertainty which spending departments in Westminster, including the Scottish and Welsh Office, expect to occur. Just as spending rounds currently vary in their tightness, Assembly finance would also fluctuate in response to the fiscal stance.

However, the analogy is not exact. It is certainly not unknown for Central Government to manipulate the fiscal stance for electoral advantage. But with Assemblies in place in different parts of the UK, Central Government might be able to manipulate the fiscal stance at different times to assist members of its party in the Assemblies. For example, the Chancellor might be persuaded to reduce excise duties on whisky in the budget prior to elections for the Scottish Assembly. One might argue that this provides a strong case for synchronising elections to the Assemblies and to Central Government, since such considerations might be a regular distraction for Central Government from the key task of maintaining a sound fiscal stance. And if the central governing party are not to have a monopoly on determining the timing of these elections, the logical extension is to have fixed term parliaments.

Whether resources are raised from tax assignment or revenue sharing, all of the schemes which have so far been proposed for the Scottish Assembly suggest that they will be insufficient to meet current levels of public expenditure without some further 'top-up' grant from Central Government. In the next section, we discuss the size of the 'equalisation grant' Whether this grant comprises a large or small proportion of all resources available to the Assembly, its existence guarantees Central Government a say over how the Assembly spends its money. However, the proportion of resources which is raised from assignment or revenue sharing creates an important *perception of ownership* which has much greater political than economic significance. Warned by Central Government that its spending plans were inappropriate, the Assembly could respond by arguing that its right to determine its own priorities was based on the large share of its total revenues assigned to it and to which it was *rightfully entitled*. How this would be resolved would depend not only on the relative size of the amounts involved, but also on the bargaining positions of the two bodies.

Council tax is the only form of localised tax in the UK at present. It is collected by local authorities and is fully assigned to them. Even though this is the case, their freedom of action is limited because council tax only contributes a small share of their total revenue. The fact that they are dependent on substantial top-up funding from Central Government reduces the scope for local initiative. This problem arises in a different guise in the next section where we discuss territorial equalisation issues.

In a sense, however, the existence of council tax provides the Assembly with additional fiscal latitude. By cutting its support grant to local authorities, it could force them to raise council tax and/or increase their borrowing. Thus, the Assembly will be able to finance enhanced service provision without any need to increase income tax. Instead the increase will be paid for by council tax payers via the local authorities. Local authorities will be anxious that they be protected from such circumstances and again an independent commission may have a protective role to play on their behalf.

Equalisation in the UK

The difference between what a territory would be assigned in specific tax receipts and what it needs to spend constitutes the equalisation grant that Central Government would have to issue in order that an agreed standard of service could be maintained, in the absence of any borrowing powers. Here we examine the size of the equalisation grant which would have been needed for the financial year 1993–94 if each territory was assigned a population-based share of UK income tax revenues and services were to be provided at the same standard as under the present Block system.

Revenue sharing is a more practical form of tax assignment because precise estimates of tax revenue in each of the UK territories are extremely difficult for many types of tax. For example, allocating income tax to a specific place of residence runs into difficulty when tax payers have residences in more than one authority or where the location of their paypoint is different from that where they work. The same is true for National Insurance contributions. Allocation of corporation tax to particular locations is extremely difficult. Are profits to be allocated to the location of the head office of a company? Or to the plants where goods are actually produced? With multi-plant companies, transfer pricing could be used to redistribute profits in the best interests of the company. Locational assignment of VAT is also highly complex. Such considerations suggest that revenue sharing presents fewer logistical problems than tax assignment.

Actual outturn figures for tax revenue and territorial spending are available for the 1993–94 financial year. Table 1 summarises General Government Expenditure (GGE) by territory and function for the 1993–94 financial year.

GGE can be broken down into two parts – identifiable and non-identifiable. Identifiable GGE is that expenditure which has been allocated to a particular territory and which has been incurred for the benefit of that territory's population. Non-identifiable expenditure, on the other hand, either cannot be identified from public records as having been incurred in a particular territory of the UK or is such that it would be misleading to attribute expenditure to particular territories since it is incurred on behalf of the UK as a whole. Unidentifiable expenditure was distributed according to 1993 population share. Scotland therefore received 8.8 per cent of unidentifiable expenditure on each service, England 83.4 per cent and so on. This proportionately allocated unidentifiable expenditure was then added to each respective country's identifiable expenditure to provide an estimate of total GGE for each territory.

Table 1: GGE by Territory and Function (£million)

Function	England	Scotland	Wales	N Ireland	TOTAL
Defence	19,081	2,013	1,144	641	22,879
Overseas Services	2,943	311	176	99	3,529
Agriculture etc.	3,006	538	290	283	4,117
Trade etc.	7,024	1,076	601	593	9,294
Transport	8,258	1,032	591	239	10,120
Housing	4,118	652	391	238	5,399
Other Environmental	6,983	1,191	643	285	9,102
Law & Order	11,971	1,271	576	1,037	14,855
Education	27,562	3,795	1,709	1,332	34,398
National Heritage	1,337	178	70	7	1,592
Health	34,871	4,601	2,354	1,339	43,165
Social Security	71,633	7,805	4,594	2,687	86,719
Miscellaneous	6,406	906	470	278	8,060

Source: Public Expenditure – Statistical Supplement to the Financial Statement and Budget Report 1995–96, HM Treasury, February 1995, Cmnd 2821

By comparing the estimated total GGE for each of the four territories with estimated revenue, it is possible to gain an indication of the size of the equalisation grants which would have been required in 1993–94, had tax assignment been used in preference to the block grants. Table 2 below details the findings.

Expressing these on a per capita basis provides an indication of relative magnitude. The required equalisation grant in England would have been £3,223 per capita, in Scotland £3,950, in Wales £3,678 and in Northern Ireland £4,548. Clearly, assignment could be extended beyond income tax to include other forms of revenue generation. This would reduce the required per capita grants, but there would still be an imbalance between the territories.

As argued above, such assignment would have political rather than economic implications. And so long as the equalisation grant is positive – that is government spending exceeds revenue in the territory – Westminster will continue to have some leverage to influence the Assembly's spending plans. As discussed in the conclusion of the last chapter, it may be necessary to protect the Assembly by placing restraints on Central Government's powers to freely vary Assembly resources.

Table 2: The Territorial Equalisation Grants for 1993–94 (£million)

Territory	Income Tax Revenue	Expenditure	Required Grant
England	48,741	205,193	156,452
Scotland	5,143	25,369	20,226
Wales	2,922	13,609	10,687
Northern Ireland	1,636	9,058	7,422

Source: as Table 1 and authors' calculations

Tax Variation Powers

The only previous example of tax-variation powers in the UK occurred early
in the life of the Stormont government when it was allowed freedom to set some
tax rates (although the major revenue-generating taxes were retained at Westminster). However, expenditure exceeded domestic revenue relatively quickly
and a grant-based system was introduced so that spending levels in Northern
Ireland did not drop well below the rest of the UK. Of course, this shifted the
balance of power in the determination of how revenue were to be spent, away
from Stormont and towards Westminster.

An alternative to the tax assignment mechanisms discussed in the previous
section is to permit Assemblies to raise their own taxes. This would increase
their accountability and freedom of action, but would erode Central Government control of macroeconomic policy. Here we consider only variations in
the rates at which existing taxes are levied, rather than the creation of new fiscal
instruments by the Assemblies. It is variations in the rates of existing taxes
which have attracted most attention from bodies such as the Constitutional
Convention.

However, there is no reason, in principle, why the Assemblies should not
introduce new instruments. For example, the Scottish Assembly might decide
to charge motorway tolls. The revenues would be paid both by Scottish
motorists and visitors to Scotland and thus not be borne exclusively by Scottish
business and households. Arguably, these would reduce the externalities associated with high traffic volumes while providing a fund for environmental
improvement or enhancement of transport infrastructure. Central Government would be suspicious of granting freedom to introduce new taxes, however,
both on the grounds of equity and efficiency and because they would represent
an unknown threat to its control over macroeconomic policy. Any prevention
of such fiscal freedom will have to be explicitly included in the legislation.

In particular, there is one area which will be of prime concern to the
business community – business rates. Following vociferous campaigning
from commerce and industry, particularly in Scotland, a unified business
rate has been applied to the whole of the UK. Business opposition to
devolution would undoubtedly increase if there was any likelihood of return
to the previous system of locally-determined business rates. Though this
would provide the Assembly with a further independent source of finance,
it is likely that the business lobby will argue for its explicit exclusion from
the Assembly legislation.

Interestingly, recent research by the IFS indicates that the incidence of
business rates did not fall most heavily on business. Instead, they were mainly
paid for by the landlords of commercial property whose rent receipts fell when
business rates rose. Who ultimately bears the burden of taxation is very relevant
to the income tax powers proposed for the Assembly as we shall now see.

The only tax variation powers so far proposed is for Scottish Assembly to
be able to vary the standard rate of income tax by plus or minus three pence
in the pound. It is not clear why this particular scale of variation has been
selected. Our previous discussion suggested that if a rigid block grant system

is introduced, Assemblies could find themselves with unplanned revenue short-falls relative to expenditure requirements. These are short-term difficulties for which tax-variation powers are not particularly suited. Changes in income tax are normally introduced only at budget time. A Scottish Assembly would have to decide very quickly after the UK budget whether to vary Scottish rates and by how much, since Central Government and the Assemblies will use the same financial year. But increased revenues would only start to flow after the start of the next financial year with some (for the self-employed etc.) being delayed until tax returns are completed after the year-end. Short-term borrowing facilities seem a much more appropriate method of dealing with unexpected revenue shortfalls or expenditure overruns.

The collection of revenues from any increase in tax rates announced by the Assembly raises a number of logistical issues. For example, how is residence in Scotland to be established? – by place of residence or location of employer? Whichever is selected would create incentives for manipulation of returns to avoid tax. The issue will be whether the benefits of such avoidance exceed its cost. Currently, wide variations in rates of council tax do not appear to have led to substantial reallocations of labour and wide variations in local income taxes in other countries, such as Denmark, do not appear to cause widespread disruption of the labour market. Nevertheless, if used to its maximum extent, an increase of 3p in the pound in the standard rate of income tax would have a significant impact on Scottish taxpayers. This is indicated in Table 3 below which shows the effect of an increase in 3p in the standard rate of income tax. The figures relate to an employed individual receiving only the single person's allowance. At its peak, the income of someone earning £500 per week would be diminished by more than 2.2 per cent.

A tax increase could be forced on the Assembly by the Treasury which, for a variety of economic and/or political reasons, might wish to reduce its equalisation grant to Scotland. This seems rather a short-term approach. The Treasury would be more likely to seek a permanent reduction in the net resources allocated to Scotland. Increasing tax rates would, as mentioned above, present logistical difficulties, might distort the labour market and could be reversed in the following financial year. For these reasons, this would not seem the appropriate method for the Treasury to effect a lasting change in resource allocations to the territories.

Table 3:   Impact of 3p Increase in Income Tax

Weekly Income (£)	Increased Tax Take (£)	As Percent of Gross Income
100	0.00	0.00%
200	2.12	1.06%
300	5.12	1.71%
400	8.12	2.03%
500	11.12	2.22%
600	12.17	2.03%
700	12.17	1.74%

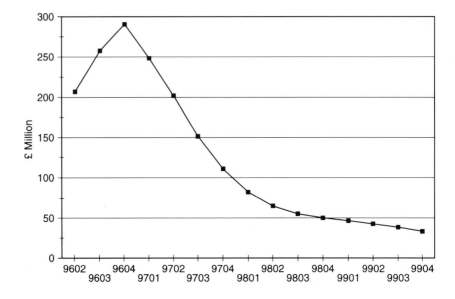

Figure 1   Tartan tax simulation: effect on GDP

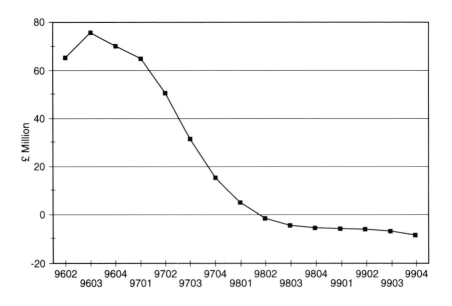

Figure 2   Tartan tax simulation: effect on consumption

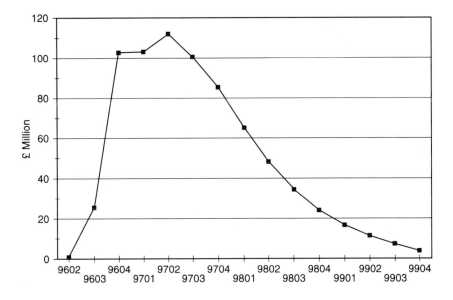

Figure 3   Tartan tax simulation: effect on investment

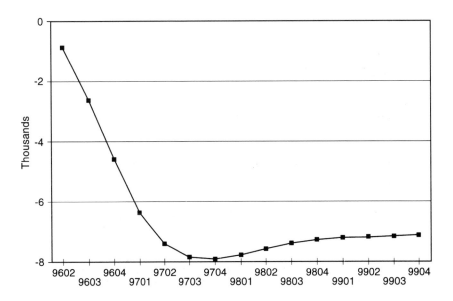

Figure 4   Tartan tax simulation: effect on unemployment

Rather, this change is more likely to be introduced by the Assembly to boost its own expenditure. It could be intended to meet shortfalls in either current or capital spending. They could fund projects which had been clearly explained, costed and approved by the Scottish electorate or used as a more general firefighting fund, to meet unforeseen contingencies. The former is clearly more likely to receive the approval of the working population than the latter.

Workers' reaction to any tax increase is crucial to its ultimate impact. In particular it will affect the incidence of the tax. If workers succeed in maintaining their real private income by demanding compensating increases in wages from employers, the incidence of the tax will be pushed on to business. In turn, employers may try to maintain their incomes by increasing prices, forcing consumers to ultimately fund the tax increase. These effects depend on the willingness and ability of workers and firms to pass the burden of the tax to others. If the uses of the funds by the Assembly are generally approved of by workers, they may feel that they are being compensated for the reduction in private income by an increase in social income. As a result, their demands for higher wages will be muted. Alternatively, Scottish workers may lack the market power to effect such wage increases or be locked into UK-wide bargaining structures to which increases in Scottish income taxes are only a minor consideration.

The worst scenario for Scottish businesses is a situation where they concede a compensating wage increase to their employees which they are then unable to pass on in the form of higher prices. In this case, they bear the entire incidence of the tax. In addition, suppliers to the domestic Scottish market may experience a downturn in demand when increased income tax reduces real disposable household expenditure.

In addition, the tax may have adverse labour supply effects, reducing the willingness of workers to provide labour. This may occur through a reduced willingness to participate in the labour market, say by older men or married women. It may result from increased migration to the rest of the UK, for example, where tax rates are lower. At least in the short-run, the evidence on labour supply and migration in the UK suggests that such effects are unlikely to be very significant.

If the income tax rise is assigned by the Assembly to specific projects which offset the increase in taxation, the net effect on the Scottish economy will be to balance out the reduction in demand stemming from higher taxes. Higher demand in some sectors will be offset by lower demand in others. Indeed, given a high propensity to import out of private consumption in the Scottish economy the net effect may well be an overall increase in the level of demand, improving prospects for many businesses

To give a rough guide to the net effects of such a tax-funded increase in spending on the Scottish economy, we use a macroeconomic simulation model of the UK economy – Compact[1]. A balanced increase in government spending and tax receipts equivalent to 3p in the pound on the standard rate is simulated

[1]We are grateful to John Ireland, University of Strathclyde for running these simulations on our behalf.

from 1996 to the end of 1999. The results which we show are essentially those from the first few years of a long-run simulation. The model has the characteristic that in the long-run, the government maintains a fixed PSBR to GDP ratio. It includes empirically-derived mechanisms to deal with the labour supply, wage and price effects described above. For example, wage bargainers strive to maintain their real incomes in response to tax increases, at least in the short-run.

In the Scottish case, the response of wage bargainers will probably depend on their view of the appropriateness of the spending increase and also their view of the length of time during which taxes will be higher. This will depend on the credibility of Assembly pronouncements about fiscal strategy. Initially this is likely to be low and may therefore lead to higher wage demands.

The results from the simulation are predicated on the assumption that the Assembly is able to increase its spending and pay for this through higher income tax. They also are based on the assumption that the spending precedes the increase in taxation. During this period there is an initial surge in activity. GDP rises (Fig 1), reaching a peak increase of £300 million two quarters after the start of the simulation. It subsequently falls back when the tax rises take effect, ending the period only slightly higher. Consumption follows a similar pattern (Fig 2) rising, then falling. The effect on investment (Fig 3) is delayed since it takes time to put capital spending plans in place. Finally, over the whole period, there is a small reduction of 8,000 in the level of unemployment (Fig 4).

This simulation must be treated with considerable caution. It is not specifically designed for the Scottish economy, though we know from many economic indicators that Scotland is fairly representative of the UK as a whole. The timing of the effects will depend critically on the nature of the projects being undertaken, which with a small economy such as that of Scotland will inevitably be 'lumpy'. What they do not suggest, however, is that a 3p in the pound increase in income tax in Scotland will have a cataclysmic effect on the Scottish economy.

Conclusion

This chapter has investigated tax mechanisms for raising finance. It has concentrated on tax assignment and revenue sharing. While in principle, differences between such tax powers and grant finance may not appear to have great economic significance, in practice, they can have an important impact on the balance of power between Assemblies and Central Government. If it is to be stable, this relationship must not clearly disadvantage one of the parties. Otherwise the electorate may not think the game worth playing and opt for more radical constitutional change. When discussing tax raising powers, council tax and business rates should not be overlooked. The Assembly may be able to force local authorities to change council tax rates to indirectly fund its own expenditure and, unless explicitly prevented from introducing new tax instruments, it may find ways of raising finance from the business sector. Finally, simulations of the proposed powers to vary income tax in Scotland do not suggest that it will have a substantial overall impact on the economy. Its effects, however, will very much depend on the spending plans which it is intended to fund and on the reaction of workers to these schemes.

6 Grant finance

Introduction

As explained in Chapter 5, there are arguments in favour of allowing a Scottish Assembly and any other regional Assemblies to have some access to tax finance. But it seems unrealistic to suppose that, initially at least, tax finance would raise more than a small proportion of any Assembly's spending requirements. So grant finance is likely to be of central importance.

This chapter looks at various aspects of grant finance. It begins by considering a fundamental choice that will have to be made in any grant scheme, namely whether grants should be allocated on a population basis, as happens to some extent with the current Block arrangements, or whether they should be allocated on some needs basis, as happens with grants to local authorities throughout the United Kingdom.

The chapter then considers how needs assessments might be made by considering briefly the arrangements used for local authorities in England and Wales and also the methodology used in a 1979 Treasury study that compared the four countries of the United Kingdom. It goes on to discuss four issues that would arise if a needs assessment approach was adopted: how should different services be weighted, how far should area's tax efforts affect their grant entitlements, who would assess the different areas' spending needs, and how often should needs be re-assessed. The chapter ends by considering some transitional arrangements which might facilitate the change from the present Block to a system of needs assessment.

Population basis or needs basis?

Since the beginning of the 1980s, funding has been allocated to the Scottish and Welsh Offices using the Barnett formula which was devised in response to the devolution debates of the late 1970s. As explained in the Chapter 4, Barnett is intended to reflect the relative population sizes of England, Scotland and Wales, though it tends to do so retrospectively. So one option for devolved Assemblies would be simply to allocate them grants that reflected a division of total approved government spending on the devolved services in accordance with the population served by each Assembly.

The main logic behind such an approach, and indeed behind Barnett, is that population is an indicator of spending needs. However, allocating grants on the basis of population alone does not seem wholly satisfactory. A major reason for this is that there are far more factors affecting needs than simply population. These factors can be broadly placed into two groups.

First, even though two areas might have similar populations, one might need more money than the other because it requires more units of input to provide a comparable level of output. For example, one area might have more schoolchildren, or more old people, or more criminals, and so need more teachers, more day centres and more policemen and women, to provide comparable levels of education, social services and law and order. Secondly, even if the areas require comparable numbers of inputs, inputs might cost more in some areas than in others. Thus island areas and inner cities might need to pay higher wages to attract staff. These two groups of factors are often referred to as differences in unit needs and differences in unit costs.

If Scotland had either sort of difference compared with the rest of the United Kingdom, then allocating funds on the basis of population would mean that service levels in Scotland would necessarily be different from those elsewhere. If the sole source of finance for Assemblies was grants, there would be reasonable grounds for complaint that, while United Kingdom citizens were everywhere paying the same tax rates, citizens were getting different service levels according to where they lived.

The situation would probably become even more serious if Scottish and other Assemblies had some access to tax revenues. For it is likely that areas with relatively high needs will have relatively low tax revenues. This is because areas with relatively large numbers of schoolchildren and old people necessarily tend to have relatively fewer people of working age and hence tend to have relatively low income and spending levels per head.

One solution to these difficulties would be to change the basis of grant allocations to one of needs. If the Assemblies relied wholly on grant finance, the mechanism could be to estimate each area's spending needs and give it an appropriate level of grant. If each area had some access to tax revenue, then the procedure could be modified to allow its tax receipts – or, if it was allowed to choose its own tax rates, its tax receipts at some standards tax rates – against its grant receipts. In essence, each area's grant, G, would be set equal to its assessed spending needs, E, less its estimated tax revenues, T.

Given that no needs assessment is made currently for Scotland and Wales versus England, it might be wondered whether the case made above for needs assessment is as strong as it seems. Certainly using populations would have three advantages over using needs: the allocation of grants would be easily understood; the allocation of grants would be stable and thus facilitate budget planning; and the allocation of grants would not be subject to a formula about which there would inevitably be much debate, some of it no doubt heated.

However, it should be borne in mind that at present Scotland and Wales secure funding well over their population proportions. These advantageous relative shares are currently being eroded gradually by the Barnett approach, and it is not clear that either country would wish to see complete convergence to population proportions.

Moreover, while few countries seek to equalise fully all differences in spending needs and tax resources, there are even fewer countries which make no effort to do so. The most notable example of a country with no formal scheme of grants designed to help low tax and high need areas is the United States. But even there, the federal government pays the states a plethora of specific grants for particular services, and at least some of these grants are intended to help the areas which most need help. So it would be eccentric for the United Kingdom to rely wholly on a population based grants system.

Of course, the United Kingdom could adopt a slightly modified population basis. For example, it could follow the approach used in a number of other countries, most notably Spain and Portugal, whereby funds are allocated to different regions or local authorities on a system that is based mostly but not wholly on population. But once the principle is conceded that grants should take account of spending needs and resource differences, it seems difficult to avoid the logical conclusion that grants should seek to eliminate the effects of such differences as far as possible. Perhaps the only caveat comes in the case of differences in costs; for it could be argued, on efficiency grounds, that these differences should be left unequalled so that people living in such areas would be encouraged, by either facing poor services or higher tax rates, to move to areas where services were cheaper. But it is not clear how much support there would be for such a policy.

In practice, though, it must be allowed that full equalisation schemes are rare. The main examples overseas are the scheme for local authorities in Sweden and the scheme for the states in Australia. But equally important examples are the schemes for local authorities within each of England, Scotland and Wales. However, the significance of these latter schemes as precedents for arrangements for devolution within the United Kingdom is somewhat weakened when it is recalled that there is no effort to equalise between local authorities in different member countries of the United Kingdom.

In view of the attractions of allowing needs to be incorporated into the grant formula, it is worth looking briefly at how needs are assessed for English and Scottish local authorities, and also at the only study – made by HM Treasury in 1979 – to assess the relative needs for spending on likely devolved services in different members of the Union.

The Standard Spending Assessment for Local Authorities in England and Wales

England and Wales have quite separate grant arrangements for local authorities, though the arrangements in each country have the same objective. The objective of the English grants is to ensure that if people in different parts of England were provided with all their local authority services at standard levels that are determined by the Central Government, then the total council tax rate set by the various tiers which serve them could equal a rate known as the council tax for standard spending (CTSS); in fact, CTSS should really be seen as a set of eight standard rates, one for each of the eight bands of property values in which each residential property is placed for council tax purposes. The Welsh system has a similar objective, but the separate arrangements for Wales mean that there, in fact, a lower set of tax rates is needed than the set needed in England to secure the same level of local government services.

The grants paid to each authority are known as Revenue Support Grants (RSG). The calculations for the grants given to an individual authority naturally depend on how many of the total raft of local services that authority provides to citizens living in its area. So, for example, a county will receive much more per head than the districts below it as counties provide most local services. The description that follows ignores the purely technical problems that arise from the existence of more than one tier by outlining how the system would work if there was only one unitary authority in each area.

In this simplified England or Wales, calculating each area's RSG would have four steps. First, the Department of the Environment or the Welsh Office would work out each area's Standard Spending Assessment (SSA) which is an estimate of the total amount of money that the area would have to spend, net of any receipts of specific grants, to provide the standard levels of services. Secondly, they would work out how much tax revenue (T) each area would secure in council tax if it set its council tax at CTSS. Thirdly, they would allow each area an equal per capita share of the proceeds of the national non-domestic rates (N). Then, finally, they would calculate each area's grant (G) as follows:

$$G = SSA - T - N$$

Thus each area could finance its services at the level assumed for SSA by setting its council tax at CTSS.

The only complex part of this exercise is working out each area's SSA. This is the sum of 13 separate SSA elements, one for each of the following 13 service blocks and sub-blocks: education (under 5, primary, secondary, post 16, other); personal social services (children, the elderly, other groups; fire services; highway maintenance; police; capital financing; other services).

The formulae used to calculate these SSAs are generally specified in terms of a sum of a series of monetary amounts multiplied by indicators of need. The various indicators reflect the demographic, physical and social characteristics of each area, and can be seen as combining a mixture of client groups and other factors. Two examples, primary schools and highway maintenance, will serve to show how the system works.

With primary schools, the SSA elements in 1994–95 relied chiefly on the numbers of primary school children, each of whom attracted an SSA allowance of £1,550.55. But other factors were also considered. For example, extra sums were allowed for children in receipt of free school meals and for areas where population densities were low so that transporting children to school was costly. In addition, it was recognised that some children require special attention or even special schools which are both very costly. But it would be inappropriate to allow specified sums for each child who was given special treatment as this would reflect varying policies as much as varying needs; so a regression analysis was conducted which showed that the incidence of children receiving such attention in different areas was explained to a significant extent by the numbers of children whose parents were single or on income support, and by the extent to which people living in the area were born outside the United Kingdom, the Republic of Ireland, the USA or the old Commonwealth; so the Standard Spending Assessment also gave weight to these various factors. Finally, an extra amount was allowed in areas of South-East England where costs were relatively high.

With highway maintenance, an area's SSA element depends on the length of roads of which it has of four different types. These types are: A roads other than trunk roads in areas with speed limits of 40 mph or less; other roads in areas with speed limits of 40 mph or less; A roads other than trunk roads in other areas; and other roads in other areas. Each road type is assigned a weight, and then a weighted total road length is calculated for each area. This SSA element chiefly allowed a certain amount of £2,356.28 per kilometre of weighted length, with extra for traffic flows above a threshold level. The SSA also allowed an extra amount for snow clearance; this amount was based on the four different types of road each weighted rather differently, and it also allowed for the average numbers of days each year on which snow is lying at 0900.

There is little use of regression analysis in estimating the roads maintenance element, but it is used in estimating many elements. Aside from any general problems with regression analyses, there is a circularity problem here in that if a group of areas with similar characteristics spend more one year, then subsequent regression analyses may suggest they 'need' to spend more. Thus regression-based analysis has been subject to criticism. But it is not easy to devise a more robust system.

The Grant-Aided Expenditure System for Local Authorities in Scotland

The system of grants to local authorities in Scotland is quite separate from the system used in England, but its general approach is exactly the same, though it is rather more complex in operation. However, the estimated figures for spending needs are called Grant Aided Expenditures (Ages) rather than Sass. The GAE for each area is estimated, as in England, by summing elements for different services. In fact, there are over 40 separate elements, some of them for services of very low total spending such as registration of births and school crossing patrols. But the indicators used bear strong similarities to those used in England as can be illustrated with reference to primary schools and highway maintenance.

Primary school costs are allowed for in the overall education GAE element. This in turn allows, inter alia, for the number of primary schoolchildren, the numbers of these in small primary schools, urban settlement patterns (as a proxy for needs for non-teaching staff and property costs), rural settlement patterns (as a proxy for transport costs), and the numbers of income support recipients (as a proxy for the number of children entitled to free school meals). Allowances are also made for extra teachers in deprived areas and areas with ethnic minorities. Requirements for special teachers are assumed to be related directly to the total number of pupils.

For highway maintenance, ages depend chiefly on weighted road lane lengths for different types of road. Extra amounts are allowed for roads built on peat if they are 600mm or less in depth and carry 20 or more commercial vehicles per day.

The 1979 Treasury Survey

The only needs assessment study made to date for all four countries of the United Kingdom was conducted by the Treasury in 1979. It was a response to the devolution debate of that time. The outcomes never influenced block grant provision and there has been no pressure, as yet, to adopt this approach for territorial allocation within the United Kingdom, but in view of its unique position, it seems worth recalling this 1979 study.

The Treasury undertook this study in consultation with the Scottish, Welsh and Northern Ireland Offices and with the Departments of Education, the Environment, Health & Social Security, Industry & Transport, the Home Office. The study covered the six main programmes that might have been devolved, namely: health and personal social services, education and libraries (excluding universities), housing, other environmental services, roads and transport (excluding railways), law, order and protective services (excluding the police)

The Treasury began with the historical evidence, examining past allocations, and found that expenditure per capita in Wales had remained closely in line with that in England but that marked variations had arisen with regard to Scotland and Northern Ireland. In Scotland and Northern Ireland, expenditure was substantially higher per capita on all programmes except Law, Order and Protective Services in Scotland.

Initially, the Treasury team liaised with individual departments to establish the practices and procedures affecting each programme in each country. A picture was built up of how each department determined its expenditure needs and of how objective information was used to determine allocations. At this stage, the Treasury concluded that most expenditure programmes could be subdivided and that the policies pursued in each subdivision were broadly similar in each country or territory, with each department following a generally common approach in relating expenditure to factors which might affect the relative cost of implementing the policies. So the Treasury prepared a list of relevant objective indicators for each expenditure block.

Most of the services in the six main programmes that the Treasury examined are provided to individuals. So the Treasury argued that the main factor which would affect the relative expenditure needs of different countries was the varying numbers of people provided with the services; the number of people concerned might sometimes be the whole population and sometimes just a part.

But allowances were also needed for other factors, such as population sparsity or the age of the buildings in which a service is provided, as these could have a significant effect on the cost of providing that service.

The next step in the Treasury study was to determine, for each relevant factor, the information that was available under consistent definitions for all four countries. Difficulties arose where information was not available on a uniform basis – in which case ad hoc adjustments were made on the advice of statisticians – and where it could not be adjusted to provide a useful direct measure – in which case proxies were chosen, such as mortality ratios to represent morbidity.

For the purposes of our report, the main conclusion that can be drawn from the Treasury study is that it supports the view that population alone is not sufficient as a guide to relative needs in different areas. This support comes not only from their procedures but also from their results which indicated that relative per capita spending needs 'to provide the same level of service as in England were': England – 100, Scotland – 116, Wales – 109 and Northern Ireland – 131.

Two Conclusions From the Three Needs Assessment Exercises

What emerges from these analyses of needs is that estimating needs requires far more indicators than population. Clearly any body that is charged with assessing needs will have to face a major exercise in deciding what indicators are most relevant for the devolved services, and in deciding, for example, how much weight to give to such indicators as population sparsity or free school meals. Whatever choices it makes will inevitably be controversial.

But such a body will also have another decision to make which is how much weight to give to the different services or activities that Scottish and other Assemblies might provide. The following sections consider in turn this question, and then the questions of what body should be entrusted to do the assessments, the effects of having devolved taxes whose rates could be varied, and how often the assessments should be made.

Any body which was asked to estimate the spending needs of a devolved Assembly would have to begin by considering what activities or services it should undertake and what levels to allow for in assessing its spending needs. It must be supposed that the Central Government will determine which services are eligible for grant support since it is paying the grants. But it is not necessary that the Central Government also determines the levels of service which are used for estimating needs assessments, even though this was assumed in the three needs assessments approaches outlined above.

There are perhaps two reasons for questioning whether this would be appropriate in the case of a Scottish Assembly and other regional Assemblies. First, such a procedure hardly seems consistent with the principle of subsidiarity. Secondly, such an approach can have paradoxical results. For example, an area might have a high need for some particular activity, say nursery education, and thus attract a high grant, but then decide not to spend very much on that activity. Indeed, the Department of the Environment's explanation of the SSA methodology is keen to stress that this element 'is not affected by the very considerable variation between authorities in the scale of provision which it is their policy to make for under 5s'. (Department of the Environment, *Standard Spending Assessments: Guide to Methodology 1995–96*, 14). Conversely, an area might have a low need for a service, and so receive little grant in respect of it even though it chose to provide that service at a high level.

A major implication of these paradoxes is that the grants may not secure the equity that they seek. To see this, take a simple example which supposes that there are only two areas, Scotland (S) and England (E), and suppose they provide only two services, X and Y. And suppose that service levels are proportional to expenditures. To provide X at some centrally ordained level might cost £120 in S and £98 in E. To provide Y at some centrally ordained level might cost £80 in S and £102 in E. Notice that, allowing for population imbalances, the average costs of providing each service across E and S as a whole at the standard levels might be £100.

If needs assessments were based on the centrally ordained levels, both S and E would be provided with an income of £200 per head, S being granted £120 in respect of X and £80 in respect of Y, and E being granted £102 in respect of X and £98 in respect of Y. But suppose each area chose to provide X at a level 25% above the standard, with a consequent reduction in Y. S would spend £150 on X, leaving £50 for Y which it would provide at a level of only 0.625 compared with the standard level. But E would spend £122.50 on X, leaving £87.50 for Y which it could provide at 0.858 of the standard level, a much higher level than S could manage.

There is an alternative approach. Instead of giving each area a needs assessment which would be the sum of money that it would require to provide its services at centrally ordained levels, it would be possible to give each area a sum of money that would enable it to provide its services at any levels it chose provided that, in aggregate, they would cost no more than £200 per head if they were supplied at these levels across E and S as a whole. If E and S as a whole had £200 per head to spend and provided X at the level chosen by S and E, the combined area would have to spend £125 on X and would thus have £75 left for Y. The level of Y which could be provided across E and S as a whole for £75 per head would cost £60 in S and £76.50 in E.

In total, then S would be allowed £150 for X and £60 for Y, making a total of £210, while E would be allowed £122.50 for X and £76.50 for Y, making a total of £199. On this approach, if S and E chose a common level of provision for X, then they would also be able to provide Y at a common level, no matter what level they chose for X. However, their grants would depend on their levels of spending on different services; so grant assessments would have to be based either on their spending decisions in a previous year or on their proposed budgets for the forthcoming year.

Note that central government would resist the extension of such a system across all Assemblies since it would imply a considerable loss of fiscal control. Use of last year's spending, for example, to determine this year's grant reduces Central Government's degrees of freedom to deal with changes in the fiscal environment brought about by cyclical fluctuations.

It may be noted that some grant schemes, such as the one used for Australian states, refer to the spending that areas would need in order to provide average levels of services rather than centrally ordained ones. This is clearly a less centralist approach than the United Kingdom's approach, but it still refuses to allow for independent decisions over service levels by different areas and thus still results in the same paradoxes and inequities.

Grants and tax rates

The discussions so far have largely ignored the possibility of subcentral taxes. If Scotland and other Assemblies were allowed access to assigned revenues or shared tax revenues, then the simplest procedure – as adopted for local authorities with the national business rate – would simply be to deduct their estimated tax receipts from their needs assessments when calculating their grants. However, there would be the question of what to do if the outturn tax receipts were different from the forecast ones. Would the grants be subsequently adjusted, or would spending levels have to adjust? This issue scarcely arises with local authorities since local tax revenues are anyway small and are easy to forecast relatively accurately. Clearly the larger any such tax receipts were as a proportion of devolved spending, the more importance would attach to the answer to this question.

If the decision was made to adjust the grant proceeds, then perhaps the simplest course would be to revise the forecast yields monthly. In practice, grant payments would no doubt be made at monthly intervals during the year, with 1/12th of the estimated total paid in the first month. If forecast receipts were revised monthly, it would be possible to adjust each month's grants to take account of the latest forecasts and thereby greatly reduce any effect of erroneous forecasts on the Assemblies.

If Assemblies have some taxes whose rates they can control, then the issue arises of whether an area's grant should be affected by its tax rate. Until the 1980s, most local authorities found that increases in tax rates led to increased grants, the philosophy being one of helping areas which made the most effort to help themselves. Then, in an attempt to cut local spending, the situation reversed, so that areas which raised their tax rates tended to find their grant receipts falling. But while a case can be advanced for either approach, there are problems with having grants that depend on tax rates. For example, the government may not want to finalise the grant formula until it knows what tax rates will be set, while the Assemblies may not want to finalise their tax rates until they know what the formula is. So it is most likely that lump-sum grants, which do not depend on tax rates, would be used.

Who should make the needs assessments?

The discussion so far has implicitly assumed that needs assessments would actually be made by the Central Government, or more accurately a government committee that might comprise representatives from the Scottish Secretary of State, the Welsh Office, the Northern Ireland Office and the Department of the Environment. But there is another possibility which would be to entrust the task to some independent body, perhaps on the lines of the Australian Commonwealth Grants Commission which produces annual reports that are used to determine equalisation grants to the states in Australia. It was set up in 1933, as a response to secessionist movements in Western Australia and Tasmania which in turn arose from dissatisfaction with fiscal inequities between the states which comprise the Australian Commonwealth.

This Commission is required to advise the Commonwealth government – that is the Central Government – on the basis by which grants to the states should be made. Its procedures have altered a little over the years, but essentially it advises that grants should be allocated so that if all the states made the same tax effort, then they could all provide services at comparable levels. The grants are based on per capita relativity factors recommended by the Commission. In 1990–91, from a general revenue grant of $17.4bn, the states of New South Wales and Victoria both made a net contribution of over $1bn to the other states in order to allow these states to provide a 'minimum need' level of service as defined by the Commission.

The justification for equalisation was based on arguments regarding the rights of all citizens to have access to certain standards of education and health. It was further argued that the principle of equal treatment of equals should apply. That is, the net impact of government policies (through taxes and charges paid and benefits and services received) on equally well-off individuals should not depend on location within Australia. The Commission became the independent mechanism which attempted to ensure that these principles were upheld.

In some respects, the task of the Commission is much easier than the question of equalising between United Kingdom local authorities because it has to deal with few areas. But in other respects its task is more complex, because it is hard to work out just how much revenue effort each state is making compared with the others. This, in turn, is because each state has considerable freedom to determine its own tax structures. Inevitably, the Commission's conclusions are criticised from time to time. But because it is an independent body, its conclusions are generally accepted with reasonably good grace. The most consistent recent opposition to the Commission has come from the two richest states, New South Wales and Victoria, who argue, quite rightly, that they would get far larger grants from the Commonwealth if the Commonwealth grants were simply allocated between states on a population basis, with no reference to tax receipts or spending needs. But their complaint is clearly more one about the need for equalisation than about the way in which it is handled.

The chief advantage of using an independent body in the United Kingdom would be that, if its members were carefully chosen, it would be seen as impartial. But one problem it would face would be deciding the standard levels of services. It could be required to assess spending needs for service levels that were centrally ordained; but this might seem to be imposing a rather centralist approach on a body that was meant to be impartial. It might instead be required to assess the spending needs that each area would have if it sought to provide services at average levels, as is essentially the procedure followed by the Commonwealth Grants commission. But perhaps it would be worth considering allowing it to assess spending needs in the light of the different areas' own priorities, as outlined in the previous section.

Whatever service levels lay behind the body's calculations, one of its first tasks would be to decide how many indicators it should take into consideration. It is tempting to assume that dozens of indicators would be needed to get a true assessment of needs, but it is probably the case that the bulk of needs are determined by a relatively small number, and that adding in numerous indicators with relatively small weights can give a rather spurious impression of great precision. Certainly the government reduced the number of indicators used in assessing the RSGs for English local authorities when domestic rates were replaced by the poll tax, and the simpler system has met with little criticism. Likewise, the 1979 Treasury study referred only to the major factors which were believed to indicate relative need, and then suggested that a simpler approach might have been no less accurate.

However, the lack of any detailed comparison of spending needs in Scotland and England means that any new assessment would be tricky, as well as potentially highly controversial. Certainly the needs of Scotland are vastly different from those of South-East England. So the chosen indicators would have to be equally applicable across the whole of the United Kingdom.

How often should needs assessments be revised?

The Department of the Environment and the Scottish Office, and indeed the Commonwealth Grants Commission in Australia, all reassess spending needs each year. This has the advantage that spending needs are kept up-to-date.

If reassessments were made less frequently, say quinquennially, then there would be sure to be some occasions when an area found that its needs had risen sharply since the last appraisal. It might then claim that it should be given some back payment to compensate it for grants which it would have received had the system been kept up-to-date. Also, there would be some areas which would find that their needs had fallen sharply since the last appraisal and which would anticipate a large fall in grant. They might complain that it would be difficult to adjust their spending downwards sharply in the course of one year, and hence they might plead for special safety net provisions to take them slowly to the new grant levels. These problems might all be more acute if the Assemblies had no tax powers to use if they felt their needs were being underestimated or to soften the blow of any sudden downturn in grants.

However, there are some arguments in favour of reassessing needs less frequently than annually. For example, annual appraisals could lead to annual arguments. Also, they could make it harder for Assemblies to plan their future budgets since they would always be uncertain about next year's grant receipts. Finally, if any data needed to be collected specially for the purposes of needs assessment, then extra costs would be incurred if this data had to be collected annually rather than less frequently.

The issue of the frequency of reassessments also impacts on the issue of what happens if the government changes the services that devolved Assemblies might provide – or at least changes the services that are provided in areas where there are no devolved Assemblies. Infrequent reviews might make it harder for the government to delete services at short notice, which could prove beneficial to Scotland if it sought to retain in the public sector a service that was being privatised in England. But equally it would be disadvantageous if some new service was provided in England and thus expected to be provided by the Scottish Assembly without its grant being increased.

Transitional Arrangements

Suppose a Scottish Assembly, or any other Assembly, is set up after the next election, and suppose it has only modest tax powers. It would be able to supply the services it takes over at their current levels only if it is given the same resources as are now devoted to those services.

In practice, this would necessarily occur only if the current Block arrangements for allocating resources were retained. But there is no reason to suppose that the current Block system for allocating resources would be retained. It seems more likely that a choice would be made to move either to a population basis or to a needs assessment basis. If this happened, the Assemblies' budgets could be significantly altered. There would be no great problem if their budgets happened to rise, but there would be real problems if they happened to be cut.

It would seem wise to consider possible transitional arrangements if the budgets were cut. Of course, if the Assemblies had ample access to devolved taxes whose rates they could set, then they could raise their tax rates and either keep them high permanently or keep them high temporarily while they gradually trimmed their spending. But it seems likely that they would have few, if any, tax powers to use.

In this eventuality, there is a case for having some temporary safety net grants. Such grants could, for example, cover a four-year period between the old system and full operation of the new system. Thus they might give to any Assembly which had to move to a lower level of funding enough extra grants that in the first four years made up for respectively 80%, 60%, 40% and 20% of its grant reduction.

When the old domestic rates in England were replaced by the poll tax, individual areas were given similar safety net grants, but these were not satisfactory. The point is that while switching taxes meant that some areas became entitled to less equalising grant and others to more, switching taxes also meant that there were considerable changes in the tax burdens faced by individual households within areas. The safety net grants to areas which lost grants admittedly helped them reduce their poll tax rates and so help all their poll tax payers, but in the process they also helped households who were gaining anyway. These grants were financed by giving lower grants to areas which were scheduled to gain grant under the new system, and thus required them to raise their poll tax rates and so harm all poll tax payers, and in this process they impacted harshly on individual households who stood to lose under the new system. Arguably, it would have been much better to apply safety nets to households, not areas, when the taxes switched; and this would have been feasible with local taxes where each household receives its own bills. Eventually, something along these lines was introduced.

However, none of these worries is really relevant to devolution, even if the Assemblies do have some tax powers which they have to use to offset falling grants, because an area which finds it grants falling and which raises its taxes in response will hurt everyone, so a safety net grant to the authority will soften the rise in taxes and help ease the pain of transition for everyone.

Conclusions

In the light of our discussion of various systems for allocating grants to sub-national authorities, it would seem that while grants to devolved Assemblies could be allocated on a population basis, the balance of arguments favours allocating grants on the basis of need.

But assessing needs more accurately requires attention to be paid to numerous indicators whose choice and relative importance will always be controversial. In assessing an area's spending needs, attention could be given to what it would cost to provide services there at centrally ordained levels or to what it would cost to provide services there at average levels. Alternatively, attention could be paid to the levels set by the authority itself. The principle of subsidiarity gives some support to the last possibility, though it would have the disadvantage that an area's grant would depend on its spending patterns in either a previous year or its budget for a forthcoming year. There are arguments for and against reassessing needs annually, but perhaps the balance of arguments favours annual reassessments.

If a Scottish Assembly, or any other Assembly, has tax receipts from a tax over whose rate it had no control, its forecast receipts would no doubt be deducted from its spending needs to calculate its grant entitlement. But problems would arise if outturn tax receipts differed from the forecast receipts. One solution would be to revise the forecasts monthly and pay the grants monthly, altering grant payments in the light of any revised forecasts. It would be possible to have grant payments that depended in some way on the tax rates any Assembly might set for taxes under its control, but it would be simpler to have grants that were independent of their tax rates.

If devolution was accompanied by a new system of allocating funds between areas, some areas would find their grants falling. There would be a case for softening the blow in these areas by some safety net grants which might be gradually phased out over a period of, say, four years.

There would also be a strong case for entrusting needs assessment to an independent body or commission on the grounds that it would be seen as politically neutral in what is potentially a highly controversial activity.

7 Loan Finance

Introduction

Negotiating a variation in block grant or in tax rates is a cumbersome and time-consuming way of dealing with unplanned revenue shortfall. An additional mechanism for ensuring that they can continue to provide effective services is for the regional Assemblies to be able to top up their grant provision and/or tax revenue through the use of borrowing powers.

The only indication of what borrowing powers might be vested in the Assemblies stems from the Scottish Constitutional Convention's discussions (1995). The Convention proposes no direct borrowing powers for the Scottish Assembly and argues that, in accordance with the principle of subsidiarity, the role of local government in service provision can be safeguarded by the continuation of present local authority borrowing powers. It is these existing powers which would constitute the primary borrowing source for the Assemblies in order that they meet any capital expenditure needs beyond the coverage of the chosen funding mechanism. No provision is suggested for borrowing to finance a budgetary deficit.

This Chapter undertakes a detailed examination of the possibilities for borrowing powers. The current provisions for local authority borrowing are outlined; these are likely to remain in place, and could in turn act as a basis for similar provisions for the Assemblies on their own account. Consideration is also given to the role that the private sector can take, through the implementation of the present Private Finance Initiative, in assisting the Assemblies to capital finance projects. In considering the ability of the Assemblies to borrow one should also consider the international issues relating to the Maastricht Treaty and debt convergence criteria. This Chapter discusses the relevance of these to the devolution debate. The possibilities are then considered for borrowing to cover temporary shortfall, borrowing to cover a current budgetary deficit, and borrowing to finance capital expenditure.

The Borrowing Powers of Local Authorities

At present it is envisaged that local authority borrowing will be the main source of territorial borrowing once the devolution plans are set in motion. Present debates indicate a desire to maintain the current status of the local authorities and so it is unlikely that their powers will change significantly. An examination of the current provisions should give an indication of what to expect in the post-devolution era.

Borrowing by local authorities is currently the major source of funding for capital works and general powers associated with such borrowing are laid out in the Local Government and Housing Act (1989) and Local Government (Scotland) Act (1975) for England and Wales and Scotland respectively. There are effectively three sources of credit which a local authority can seek:

(1) an overdraft from the Bank of England or any other bank authorised under the Banking Act (1987);
(2) borrowing from the National Debt Commissioners or the Public Works Loan Board or
(3) loan instruments such as bills, bonds, mortgages, debentures or annuities.

Local authorities are not permitted to borrow from non-UK lenders or in currency other than sterling without first gaining the prior consent of the Treasury. One way of avoiding the question of foreign finance and thus not restricting the ability of the local authorities to utilise every available source of finance is through the use of the Consolidated Loans Fund (CLF). For administrative convenience the authorities usually 'pool' their loans into the CLF. The service accounts borrow from the Fund to finance capital expenditure, whilst the Fund borrows from the government to meet the demands of these service accounts. The government has no restrictions on whether it uses domestic or foreign sources to raise capital.

The CLF has the advantage of allowing authorities to borrow over the long term without the need to match each transaction to each asset. For example, assume that an authority wants to borrow a sum of money over a thirty year period to finance the building of a new hospital. Rather than pay for the asset over its lifetime, the authority may initially take a loan for five years and at the end of that period repay the loan and make a decision whether to replace that loan with another for, say, three or ten years. At the end of the thirty years the loan could have been rolled over several times. With the CLF, it is possible to take a mix of long term and short term borrowing, some at fixed and others at variable rates of interest.

For each authority a credit ceiling is calculated as its net credit liabilities at 1 April; this ceiling may be positive, zero or negative. Then credit approvals are made for specific capital expenditures. Finally, there is provision for using a proportion of capital receipts (e.g. from sales of council housing) to finance capital expenditure. Legislative provisions limit the total debt (borrowing plus other credit) that an authority can have at any one time to be not in excess of the sum of:

– its credit ceiling at the previous 1 April,
– its temporary revenue borrowing limit,
– its temporary capital borrowing limit,

- the difference between approved investment and cash and useable capital receipts,
- and any credit approvals used during the financial year.

The temporary revenue and capital limits allow the authority to borrow if it pays its creditors faster than it receives income from its debtors. Any shortfall which arises from the authority setting its charges at too low a level cannot be recouped through borrowing.

The main direct issue for devolution is the discretion a regional Assembly would have over credit approvals for local authorities. If the Assemblies are given jurisdiction over education, for example, then it would follow that credit approvals for local authority capital projects in education would be part of that function. Yet Westminster would want to retain control over borrowing totals for purposes of macroeconomic policy in general, and particularly in order to meet the Maastricht limits on total government borrowing in the UK as a whole.

However, the Assemblies would have responsibility for servicing local authority debt. This would need to be taken into account in any needs assessment exercise. To the extent that any territory's local authority debt is relatively high, this would alter the relative size of the funding allocation. Relatively larger use of public housing in Scotland, has left it with relatively large interest charges.

Government Borrowing, Macroeconomic Policy and the Maastricht Treaty

It has been the predominant presumption of the devolution discussions that control of macroeconomic policy should remain the remit of Central Government. During recent decades, such policy has increasingly concentrated on maintaining stable monetary conditions and controlling the government deficit.

These are not the only macroeconomic goals which governments might wish to follow. Past objectives have included full-employment and rapid growth. These are now viewed as responding to microeconomic, as well as to macroeconomic policies. A good example are microeconomic policies designed to increase flexibility and mobility in the labour market. This implies that, even if macroeconomic policy is seen to be the preserve of Westminster, its success may be influenced by the activities of the Assembly. For example, training provision which is likely to be the responsibility of the Assembly (Scottish Constitutional Convention 1995) will be viewed as contributing to the effectiveness of the overall effort to reduce unemployment.

Yet another approach is to consider a nation's macroeonomic performance in terms of regional composition. For example, one region may be overheating relative to the others. The ideal policy solution may then not be higher national interest rates, but more regionally-selective measures, such as a regional redistribution of government capital expenditure programmes. The outcome would be reduced national unemployment in addition to reduced national inflation. The issues are thus not simply related to equity – some regions bearing an undue proportion of the costs of macroeconomic policy – but also the effectiveness of policy. This view is embodied in the institutional arrangements for policy-making in many federal states. For example, the central banking system in the United States has a federal structure allowing for regional input into national monetary policy. Indeed this model is being followed in the design of the European System of Central Banks, where each member central bank has an input to the design of European monetary policy. While this argument has not had much prominence in the devolution debate, the creation of Assemblies might focus attention on the regional consequences of national macroeconomic policy. It would therefore be advisable to have a consultative mechanism whereby the Assembly could have an input into the design of national policy.

The criteria for joining the European Monetary Union include price stability, interest rate stability and exchange rate stability, as well as low levels of government borrowing and low stocks of outstanding government debt. These would have the direct effect of limiting the total of public sector borrowing, as well as indirect effects on the budget through attempts to maintain price, interest rate and exchange rate stability. The value of the block grant may thus be limited due to external pressures on Westminster.

In particular, Article 104b to the Maastricht Treaty laid out the fiscal convergence criteria for monetary union in the EC. In accordance with this member states should avoid excessive government deficits. The definition of excessive was laid out in the form of two criteria:

(1) the ratio of planned or actual government deficit to GDP be no greater than 3 per cent at market prices and
(2) the ratio of government debt to GDP should not exceed 60 per cent at market prices (a higher figure would be accepted if the ratio is sufficiently decreasing and steadily approaching 60 per cent).

The Maastricht criteria become relevant to the devolution debate in that, given the maintenance of power at Westminster over all matters European, it would be the UK government, not the regional Assemblies, which would be responsible for meeting these guidelines. Thus the Westminster government is accountable to the EU for maintaining its government borrowing within the agreed limits. National borrowing is, as its name suggests, a national issue and so, in accordance with a generally agreed principle, the associated powers should be retained with the UK government. As such at least some control over national borrowing must be maintained at the centre.

The simplest means of avoiding conflict between Westminster and the Assemblies is to retain primary borrowing powers at Westminster and to assign proportions of this borrowing to the territories as necessary. Funds for local projects can be augmented through local authority borrowing in conjunction with the territorial Assemblies, just as it is conducted now between the local authorities and the Scottish Office, for example.

But the Maastricht limitations on government borrowing will compound the effect of the constraints imposed by macroeconomic policy on the Assembly's freedom to design policies (as otherwise entailed in an application of the principle of subsidiarity).

The Private Finance Initiative

Possibilities for regional Assembly financing of capital projects have recently been expanded by the emergence of the Private Finance Initiative (PFI). The PFI is designed to enable the public and private sectors to work in closer harmony and in doing so to provide a more cost-effective service to the public. It is reasonable to assume that the PFI would still be in operation after the creation of the Assemblies, given the Labour Party's open pledge to develop the concept of public-private co-operation in capital ventures, and so the role that the scheme would play in future capital expenditure projects deserves discussion.

It is the intention of the Treasury that the PFI be involved in as many government capital expenditure programmes as possible. In November 1994 this was reiterated by the Chancellor of the Exchequer in his speech to the CBI Annual Conference:

'... the Treasury will not approve any capital projects unless private finance options have been explored. This will maximise the scope for, and use of, private finance while concentrating inevitably finite public capital provision on those areas where, for whatever reason, private finance is not possible.'

According to current proposals, the Assemblies must fund any capital projects out of their existing funding allocations. By embracing the rationale of the PFI, resources could be freed for other programmes and therefore assist in providing an improved standard of service. If the Assemblies could rely on private sector assistance, be it in whole or part, for capital projects, it would have a greater proportion of its funding allocation available to address these other spending priorities. By this means it may be possible for the Assemblies to fund projects which might otherwise not proceed. The fundamental points of the Initiative are that:

(1) the private sector must genuinely assume risk;
(2) there should be competition where the government facilitates a project or seeks private sector partners and also where the government purchases services as a customer;
(3) the Initiative applies not only to infrastructure projects but also to other capital investment which provides services to the public sector.

The key rationale of the Initiative is, after all, to improve the quality and value of public services and it is the government's belief that this can best be achieved through competitive market forces. In addition to the issue of whether control lies in the hands of the private or public sector there is therefore the question of whether infrastructure has been improved, industry is made more competitive or public services made more efficient as a result of the Initiative.

In pursuing the Initiative the Assemblies would have to take account of the same factors which Central Government recognise as important to the validity of private provision of capital goods. Two tests should be applied to decide whether private finance is appropriate:

1. is it possible genuinely (and satisfactorily) to transfer control and the associated risks to the private sector without disproportionate cost? and
2. can value for money be demonstrated?

In relation to point 2. the Assemblies should consider whether, if a project would have gone ahead with public finance on a similar timescale, private finance represents value for money relative to the publicly financed alternative.

In the event of control over the Private Finance Initiative being handed down to the regional Assemblies, the government's contribution would come from the Assemblies' funds. Assistance may take the form of concessionary loans, equity, transfer of existing assets, ancillary or associated works or some combination of these. The Assembly may also contribute in terms of initial planning or a straight grant subsidy.

To encourage participation in the scheme the Assemblies would need to offer attractive financial packages to the private sector.

Assembly Borrowing on its Own Account

Provision might be necessary for an Assembly to borrow to meet temporary shortfalls in revenue due to a mismatching over the financial year of the timing of revenue and expenditure. Indeed the 1978 proposals included the proposal for a Scottish loan fund to be set up for such a purpose.

At present, such an arrangement is not necessary for the Scottish Office (or, similarly for the Welsh Office and the Northern Ireland Office). The block transfer is made at the start of the financial year, paid into the Paymaster General's Office account and is drawn down during the year. The Scottish Office may choose to hold the transfer with commercial banks, but in practice only uses commercial banks for some specific purposes, like local transactions and international transactions. An Assembly might take a different view, seeing advantages in holding much of its funding from Westminster with commercial banks in Scotland. These advantages would include:

(1) the greater financial independence of placing revenues itself;
(2) the political advantage of supporting Scottish banks;
(3) and the scope for using bank deposits as leverage in encouraging Scottish banks to act in a way which was supportive of social or industrial policy in Scotland.

Whether there was a need for borrowing during the year would depend on the funding arrangements. If funding was by block grant, it would presumably result in a transfer at the beginning of the financial year, as at present. But if funding were at least in part through tax-based revenues, these might be spread over the financial year, raising the possibility of temporary shortfalls in liquidity simply due to mismatch between revenue and expenditure. The possible mechanisms for dealing with such shortfall would be:

(1) If payments continue through the Paymaster General's Office, there would have to be some agreement that temporary short-falls would be covered presumably with some safeguards to ensure that the shortfalls were indeed temporary;
(2) If payments were to be transferred to commercial bank ac-counts, overdraft facilities could be arranged;
(3) A special fund could be set up to meet such contingencies.

But there are two arguments for further borrowing powers on the part of the Assembly itself, i.e. for the Assembly to borrow to finance a deficit over the financial year as a whole. At present, if the Scottish Office has to meet unexpected expenditure which, other things being equal, would mean a revenue shortfall, then there are three possibilities. One is to draw on the general UK government reserve. But this is a last resort, particularly in the current climate of budgetary restraint. Another possibility is to negotiate an additional trans-fer through supplementary estimates to make up the shortfall. The third possibility is to reallocate expenditure within the agreed block. But the over-riding principle is that the Scottish Office should balance its budget.

But, as the discussion of the Block Grant, tax variation and tax assignment indicated, the Assembly's revenue sources may, unintentionally, not meet expenditure requirements. A simple formula for the Block Grant may not adequately capture changing expenditure conditions, and tax revenues may fall short of expectations. Under the current system, since the Scottish Office is financed through internal allocation, there is considerable scope for flexibil-ity, notably through bypass payments. Further, if in aggregate expenditure exceeds revenue, the UK government has the power to borrow to make up the shortfall. But, without some provision for borrowing, any shortfall for an Assembly could only be covered by four possible course of action:

(1) An ad hoc additional transfer from Westminster. Logistically such a transfer would be possible, but politically it could be damaging to the public perception of the working of devolu-tion.
(2) Pushing the problem onto the local authorities by reducing their allocation from the Assemblies
(3) Borrowing by the Assembly. For macroeconomic policy pur-poses, Westminster would want to set limits on any such borrowing. In any one year the Assembly might be limited to borrowing by some ceiling percentage of total expenditure; there could be a requirement of a balanced current budget on average over, say, a five year period. There could be limits on the type of borrowing allowed along similar lines to the local authorities' limits.
(4) Drawing on the loan fund. If it were adequately resourced, such

a fund could allow current budgetary deficits in downturn years, to be matched by surpluses in upturn years.

Again, Westminster might want to impose some limits on this type of borrowing by Assemblies to allow macroeonomic policy goals to be met. But the provisions for local authority borrowing provide adequate precedent for arrangements for controlling the amount of borrowing, the purposes for which it is required, and the instruments by which it is effected. If the end result of borrowing to assist industrial expansion, for example, is lower needs in the territory, then the Exchequer should gain from reduced block grants in the future.

Transitional Arrangements

The establishment of an effective system for day-to-day financing may well be one of the most important elements in arrangements for the transition to a fully-devolved system of government. The internal mechanisms suitable for a system of only administrative devolution are inadequate for a system of legislative devolution, where financing mechanisms will lack flexibility. There are questions of principle to be addressed: the division of control over local authority borrowing; whether the Assembly should organise its own banking; and whether it should be allowed to borrow, and under what conditions. But the immediate issue would be how to protect the Assembly from unanticipated shortfalls. Indeed the issue is likely to be greatest in the transitional period, as new funding mechanisms are put into place. The important issue then would be whether such arrangements should be set up internal to the Westminster system, i.e. through existing funds, or externally to it in the form of a Scottish Loan Fund.

Conclusion

The consensus that there should be no Assembly borrowing powers has diverted attention from a range of important issues, many of which arise from the fact that there are three distinct needs which borrowing might address, each of which might warrant different borrowing mechanisms: borrowing to cover temporary shortfalls, borrowing to cover a current budgetary deficit, and borrowing to finance capital expenditure.

The first issue refers to the status quo of local authority borrowing. Since local authorities will come under Assembly jurisdiction, some mechanism will have to be worked out to balance Assembly priorities in terms of approval for particular borrowings, and Westminster priorities in terms of total government borrowing. This issue is further complicated by the Maastricht requirements to keep borrowing within very narrow limits.

For the Assembly itself, a mechanism may be required to cover shortfalls within the financial year, although this will depend on the nature of the funding mechanism, and thus the timing of revenue receipts. An Assembly might want to have, and exercise, the power currently enjoyed by the territorial Offices to place deposits with commercial banks. But there might also be justification for setting up a special loan fund.

The justification for such a fund becomes stronger when we consider the possibility of shortfall over the financial year as a whole. Such a shortfall may arise simply from the inevitable lesser flexibility of a funding mechanism for devolution, i.e. it may be unintentional, resulting from inadequate mechanisms to cater for unforeseen eventualities. But it may also arise from a deliberate attempt at stabilisation policy in the territories, particularly if it was judged that UK macroeconomic policy was not well-tuned to the economic conditions in any one territory. The loan fund would then need to be large enough to cover deficits in downturn years, to be recouped from surpluses in upturn years.

Third, there is the case for borrowing to finance capital projects, although the case is mitigated somewhat by the Private Finance Initiative, which would encourage Assemblies to raise private sector finance. But, if capital projects are intended to improve economic conditions in the territory, they will in due course generate increased tax revenue and reduce the block grant as determined by relative needs. Taking the long-term picture, therefore, such borrowing need not run against attempts by Westminster to reduce borrowing. The Assemblies could borrow through the same pooling mechanism as the local authorities; but they might find a ready market for a range of borrowing instruments.

There is therefore a wide range of issues of principle to address with respect to borrowing, as well as issues of practice, as to the best mechanisms to set up for the purpose.

8 Summary and Review

The purpose of this report was to consider current thinking on the financing of devolution and to raise questions of principle as well as of logistics of implementation which have yet to be addressed.

While there has been a considerable degree of administrative devolution, the current proposals are for legislative devolution, in Scotland, Wales, Northern Ireland and the English regions. The discussions are most advanced for Scotland, with some cross-party agreement having been established in the Constitutional Convention. The focus here has therefore been on Scotland as the first territory in which legislative devolution is likely to occur. But the likelihood of the extension to the other territories of the system applied to Scotland must be borne in mind.

The majority of proposals over the last twenty years for financing devolution have focused on funding by block grant. But the possibility of tax-based finance has also been on the agenda. The Constitutional Convention in Scotland has proposed that the Assembly have the power to change the rate of income tax by up to 3p in the pound. The Liberal Democrats have advocated more extensive tax-based financing in Wales. But Northern Ireland's experience of financing by tax revenues raised in the province, in the period 1920–72, has highlighted the importance of ensuring that financing arrangements take adequate account of expenditure needs.

The first consideration is what is to be financed and what freedoms and distribution of powers are to be allowed for in financing arrangements. This question is further complicated by the change underway in division of responsibilities between the public and private sectors. Again any funding arrangements would need to be flexible enough to address the evolution of political ideas on that front. At the same time, there needs to be a recognition that Assemblies will not in general mirror the political priorities of Westminster, so that the division of powers should explicitly address how differences of view as to the allocation of expenditure responsibilities is to be handled.

There are various possible mechanisms for addressing the issues raised by the division of responsibility over service provision:

- Make the range and level of services to be financed absolutely explicit, with provision for periodic review.

- Provide Assemblies with their own revenue-raising capabilities to allow for regional differences in level and extent of service provision.

- Set up an independent body to arbitrate over disputes over service provision which is to be covered by the financing arrangements. This body might similarly arbitrate over disputes between Assemblies and local authorities over service provision and its finance.

Issues of policy difference between Westminster and an Assembly might arise over issues related to the regulation of industry. There may be a case for Assembly regulation powers in particular cases. But, particularly if full regional devolution is planned for the UK, the logistics of multi-regional regulatory differences would be very unwieldy. Yet Assemblies would have legitimate areas of concern on regulatory issues.

- Consideration should be given to setting up a mechanism whereby Assembly interests on regulatory issues could be injected into policy-making discussions at Westminster.

Similar issues of dispute over service provision are likely to arise between the Assembly and local authorities. Particularly given the Constitutional Convention's co-operative approach to service provision, some mechanisms would need to be considered to resolve these disputes too, and to allow local authorities some flexibility in service provision.

- Consideration should be given to setting up an independent arbitration body to resolve disputes between the Assembly and local authorities.

The block grant is the dominant proposal for Assembly finance (together with minor tax variation powers). The principle behind the current system of block funding is convergence on per capita equality. But in practice the Barnett formula has not achieved per capita equality, so that any strict application of the principle to a Scottish Assembly would result in a significant cut in funding. The case against such a basis for the block grant is that needs in Scotland are relatively great, and are under-represented by population size. If there were to be insistence on the population principle, there would need to be a gradual approach to such a basis for funding.

If, instead, the block grant is to be determined at least in part on the criterion of need, then further issues need to be addressed. The first issue is whether the aim is to provide enough finance to provide a particular (minimum, or alternatively, average) level of services according to standards established by Westminster. Unless there was specific agreement to do so, there would be no compulsion on the territories to provide that level of service (more or less might be provided). An alternative, therefore, in line with the principle of subsidiarity, would be for Assemblies to decide on their expenditure priorities, and for the financing mechanism to accommodate them.

How the needs assessment should be conducted is clearly a large question. The precedents set by the Treasury exercise and by local authority funding were considered in some detail. Assessing needs will require attention to be paid to numerous indicators where choice and relative weight will inevitably be controversial. In particular, it would have to be decided whether the needs referred to the size of the client base alone, or also reflected differential costs of providing services in each territory. On balance it seems that there might be a strong case for a relatively simple exercise. But even so the basis for the needs calculation requires detailed investigation, particularly if the principle of subsidiarity introduces new areas of expenditure into the calculation. Subsidiarity, further would suggest that the level of service to be provided would be determined by the Assembly

The third issue would be whether or not the amount of the block grant should be independent of any tax-based source of funding. A particular issue would be whether the two sources of revenue were designed to meet a specified level of expenditure, so that any increase in tax revenue would be offset by a reduction in block grant. Further, if the grant was based on estimates of tax revenues which proved to be wrong, some flexibility would be required to adjust the grant accordingly.

Fourth there is the question of who should be responsible for the assessment exercise, and how frequently the exercise should be conducted. It would seem advisable again to have an independent body responsible for needs assessment, or at least to arbitrate in cases of dispute. The frequency of exercise is a matter of deciding on the trade-off between greater frequency (say annually) to reflect changing conditions, and lesser frequency (say quinquennially) to provide a stable planning horizon. Thus to summarise our arguments on funding, we would argue:

- that the Block Grant should take account of relative need, rather than weighting the population equally;

- that the formula for the Block Grant should incorporate convergence to equality of funding relative to need;

- that where the convergence principle means a reduction in funding, the adjustment should occur more gradually during weak economic conditions;

- that the formula should be transparent but allow for flexibility in the light of changing conditions of need;

- that needs assessment exercises should be carried out by an independent body;

- that if a needs assessment implied a significant drop in funding, there should be a phased adjustment to the new level of funding over, say, five years.

There is a current proposal for freedom to add three pence to income tax for Scotland. This is only one of a range of possibilities. The relative merits of alternative forms of tax assignment and revenue sharing are discussed in Chapter Five. The consensus seems to be that income tax is the simplest tax to assign. However, even if there is agreement on this proposition, further issues need to be addressed. In particular, is the extra revenue to be calculated by means of a simple estimate (e.g. population share of total revenue) or by a taxpayer-by-taxpayer calculation based on some definition of residence. Simplicity and absence of tax avoidance would suggest the former. Further, there is no particular reason why the three pence maximum should have been chosen.

However, politically it would probably be difficult now to propose a higher ceiling.

It would have been possible to plan for a much higher proportion of funding to be tax-based, in order to increase accountability. This possibility is also considered in Chapter Six. But it would require some top-up grant since no one tax, or subset of total taxes, is likely to cover total expenditure. The issues raised by the top-up grant are the same as for full block-grant funding, except that it is likely to be more highly politically charged, being seen (and possibly misunderstood) by the public as a subsidy.

At the moment there is no proposal for borrowing powers for the Assembly. The expectation is that borrowing would be confined to what is provided for under the current system (local authorities etc.). However, since the Assemblies would be responsible for local authorities, and the servicing of their debt, it would need to be established whether or not the Assemblies would have the power of approval over this debt.

Because the Maastricht Treaty imposes limits on total government borrowing, Westminster has the responsibility to determine the total. But this need not rule out the possibility of Assembly borrowing, which could be subject to controls similar to the local authorities. Indeed, because of the interdependence between regions and the nation as far as outcomes are concerned, the Assembly is unlikely to be content to leave macro issues, of which government borrowing is only one, to Westminster.

The 1978 proposals for devolution in Scotland had included the proposal that a Scottish Loan Fund be established to cover day-to-day mismatches in revenues and expenditures. How far such mismatches would occur would depend on the timing of revenue receipts over the financial year; something like the present system with the Block being transferred at the start of the year would mean that liquidity should not be a problem. Nevertheless, Assemblies might choose to have more independence in their day-to-day financial arrangements:

- they might find advantages in operating through their own accounts with local banks;

- they would require a local fund (e.g. a Scottish Loan Fund) to provide for temporary liquidity difficulties, rather than employing any of the existing arrangements internal to Westminster.

But there are two cases to be made for additional borrowing powers. First, there is considerable scope for funding to be inadequate for a whole variety of reasons – including miscalculation, particularly in the early stages of a new funding mechanism, and unexpected calls on revenue which currently are met with by-pass payments. Second, further shortfalls could arise from changes in Westminster policy which have knock-on effects on the Assembly.

The following are mechanisms by which Assemblies might deal with budgetary imbalance in the financial year as a whole:

- Renegotiate the Block Grant.

- Draw on an existing Westminster funding mechanism such as the Consolidated Loan Fund.

- Draw on a Scottish Loan Fund.

- Issue securities on the external market.

All except the first option would require some agreement on overall borrowing limits for macroeconomic purposes. There could be agreement for this type of borrowing to average zero over, say, five years.

Second, there is a case for Assembly borrowing on its own account to finance capital expenditure. Otherwise, any capital expenditure not done by the local authorities, or e.g. hospitals, as under current arrangements, would need to be funded through the Private Finance Initiative or from current revenue. Again there would need to be some agreement to limits on such borrowing, for UK macroeconomic reasons, but it is not at all clear why such a possibility should be ruled out altogether.

- Assemblies could be empowered to raise finance for capital projects (subject to approval, e.g. on the lines of local authorities).

- Assemblies might see advantages in issuing their own debt securities.

Bibliography

Central Statistical Office (1995) 'Population Trends', HMSO

Department of the Environment (1994) 'The Local Government Finance Report (England) 1994–95', HMSO

Foot, M (1976) 'The Scotland and Wales Bill', HMSO

Heald, D (1994) 'Territorial Public Expenditure in the United Kingdom', Public Administration, 72, pp. 147–175

King, D (1976) 'The Fiscal Implications of Devolution', Institute for Fiscal Studies

Lynch, M., (1991) 'Scotland: A New History', Pimlico

Mitchell, J (1991) 'Scottish Public Finances', mimeo

Royal Commission on the Constitution (1973) 'Report', HMSO

Royal Commission on the Constitution (1973) 'Memorandum of Dissent', HMSO

Scottish Constitutional Convention (1994) 'Further Steps: Towards a Scheme for Scotland's Parliament', mimeo

Scottish Constitutional Convention (1995) 'Key Proposals for Scotland's Parliament', mimeo

Treasury, HM (1979) 'Needs Assessment Study – Report', HMSO

Appendix 1 : The Development of Administrative/Executive Devolution in the UK (1707–1970)

We follow a broadly chronological approach in discussion the development of devolved powers in the UK, considering the territories separately. Most of the significant changes have taken place in Scotland. However, for different reasons, Northern Ireland provides some interesting lessons because it did, for a time, experience legislative devolution; the experience there with financing by means of tax assignment is of particular interest in the current debate.

Scotland

Pressure for devolution of power in the UK can be traced back to the origins of the British state. In 1707, following the Union of the Parliaments, special arrangements were made for the conduct of government business in Scotland, with the appointment of a Secretary of State. The post was abolished after the second Jacobite Rebellion in 1745 and between 1745 and 1885, no government minister had exclusive responsibility for Scotland. Scottish affairs were handled by the Home Office during that time. Much of the effective political power in Scotland was held by the Lord Advocate for Scotland.

The immediate post-Union period has perhaps most relevance to the current position with many of the major interest groups in Scotland, such as the church and the nobility, feeling that their expectations of the Union had not been realised. An attempt to revoke the Union in 1713 failed narrowly and Scottish politics took around 40 years to come to a grudging acceptance of the Union (Lynch, 1991, pp. 318–326).

In 1885 the role of Secretary for Scotland was created with the incumbent generally being a member of Cabinet. The powers devolved to the Secretary were wide-ranging and included *law and order* and *education*. These responsibilities continued to broaden prior to the First World War with *agriculture*, *fisheries*, *local government* and *prisons* and then, in 1919, *health* being added to the remit.

The role was upgraded to Secretary of State for Scotland in 1926, and then in 1939 the Scottish Office relocated to Edinburgh from London. Further

expansion of the powers of the Secretary of State followed. Since 1954 these
have included *animal health policy, highways, electricity, road passenger transport, ancient monuments, royal parks and palaces.* In 1962, all of these
responsibilities were reorganised and brought within four departments of the
Scottish Office – Agriculture and Fisheries, Development, Education and
Home and Health. A fifth department was added in 1973 – originally called
the Scottish Economic Planning Department, later to become the Industry
Department. This was responsible for taking over the role of the DTI in
Scotland and for administering the other economic activities with which the
Scottish Office was involved.

During this century, there has thus been a substantial increase in the
administrative power of the Scottish Office. Many of the major programmes
of government – education, health, law and order, local authorities – are now
administered within Scotland. However, these programmes are those of the
majority party at Westminster and the policies may not reflect majority
opinion within Scotland. For the last 16 years, the tensions caused by a
predominance of Conservative MPs in Westminster determining policy in
Scotland, where there is a clear Labour majority, have been very evident. The
fact that these policies have been based on conviction rather than consensus
politics have served only to add to this pressure.

Wales

The process of administrative devolution in Wales lagged well behind that in
Scotland. The Welsh Office and the role of Secretary of State for Wales only
came into being in November 1964. Before this there existed an office of the
Minister for Welsh Affairs, this role being held at first by the Home Secretary
and later by the Minister of Housing and Local Government.

The Welsh Office took over virtually all the functions in Wales of the
Ministry of Housing and Local Government , namely:

Housing	*Water*	*Town & country planning*
Sewerage	*Local government*	*Economic planning*
Roads		

At present, the Secretary of State for Wales also has authority to exercise
oversight within Wales on matters of national policy dealt with by the Minis-
tries of Agriculture, Fisheries and Food, Health and Transport and the
Departments of Education and Employment and the Board of Trade.

Thus, substantial additions have been made to the responsibilities of the
Welsh Office which now include: the health service, forestry and agriculture,
ancient monuments, tourism, child care and primary and secondary education. The Welsh Office and the Secretary of State are thus now responsible
for most matters dealt with in England by the Department of the Environment or, in the case of primary and secondary education, the Department
of Education.

Northern Ireland before 1920

The Act of Union (1800) provided for the abolition of the Irish Parliament and for Irish representation in both Houses at Westminster. As in Scotland the immediate post-union period was one of turmoil and by 1830 there were strident calls for the Act to be repealed. However, the support for repeal was not unanimous. The Protestants wanted to remain in the union, fearing a new Irish parliament which included Catholics would make them the oppressed minority in a Catholic-dominated Ireland.

Calls for Home Rule gathered momentum in the mid 19th Century, following the potato famine. The inadequate famine relief measures of the British government added a new element of bitterness to Irish nationalism. Home Rule, which would set up an Irish parliament to deal with Irish matters whilst Westminster would deal with affairs of the Crown and Government, began to be widely supported. At the 1885 General Election the Irish home rule candidates held the balance of power between the Liberal government and the Conservative opposition.

In 1886 Gladstone introduced the first of many Home Rule Bills. It was not, however, until 1914 that one such Bill was passed by both Houses of Parliament, but the advent of war meant that it was never enforced. In 1916 the leaders of the Easter Rebellion in Dublin issued a proclamation declaring an Irish Republic but the rebellion was quashed. The execution of all the signatories to the proclamation did, however, mobilise Irish public opinion in support of the cause.

In 1920 legislative devolution was introduced to Northern Ireland with the establishment of the Stormont Parliament. Because of its significance, this more recent Northern Irish history is discussed in detail in Chapter 2.

Appendix 2 : The Barnett formula

The Barnett formula expression is derived by using the product rule to evaluate the change in the ratio of Scottish to English expenditure x_S/x_E.

$$\frac{\partial \left(\frac{x_S}{x_E} \right)}{\partial t} = \frac{1}{x_E} \frac{\partial x_S}{\partial t} - \frac{x_S}{x_E^2} \frac{\partial x_E}{\partial t} \tag{1}$$

which can be expanded to

$$= \frac{1}{x_E} \frac{\partial x_S}{\partial x_E} \frac{\partial x_E}{\partial t} - \frac{x_S}{x_E^2} \frac{\partial x_E}{\partial t} \tag{2}$$

The relative rate of change of expenditure in Scotland is given by $\partial x_S/\partial x_E$ and this is determined by the Barnett or Portillo factor, φ.